1 MONTH OF
FREE
READING

at
www.ForgottenBooks.com

By purchasing this book you are eligible for one month membership to ForgottenBooks.com, giving you unlimited access to our entire collection of over 1,000,000 titles via our web site and mobile apps.

To claim your free month visit:
www.forgottenbooks.com/free1119792

ISBN 978-0-331-84687-4
PIBN 11119792

BRADLEY UNIVERSITY PEORIA, ILLINOIS
VOLUME 24

*Seek the self
within the dawning
of our knowledge*

Life is before us . . .

only once can we
live it!

CLASS OF 1928.

Do we peer inside
and do nothing?
Is there any peace in silence?

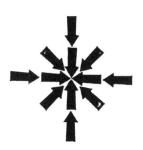

Shall we reflect the
growing apathy
or strive to be?

The self . . .

preserves

our memories

THIS STORE IS OWNED AND
OPERATED BY THE UNIVERSITY FOR
THE CONVENIENCE OF THE ENTIRE
UNIVERSITY COMMUNITY.
    ANY MONIES DERIVED FROM THIS
OPERATION ARE TURNED BACK TO THE
GENERAL OPERATING FUND OF THE UNI-
VERSITY TO HELP DEFRAY COSTS OF THE
STUDENTS' EDUCATION.

Combining them to form
within our knowledge

a *time of confidences,*
a *time of solitude,*

Yes, the self is a boundless,
measureless sea,
to be found inside
each of us.

McGovern, Nimoy draw large crowd

GESTURING for emphasis, Leonard Nimoy explains the reason for the program's delay. He soon left to help retain the group which had to wait three hours for the senator's arrival.

ONE thousand people jam to the front of the Student Center Ballroom for free handshakes.

18

BEFORE Illinois' primary, George McGovern speaks in the Student Center about his future plans of United States withdrawal from Vietnam.

Plays and concerts fill weekends
at close of '72 spring semester

SPRING concerts featured Curtis Mayfield,
War, Manasas, Taj Mahal, Beautiful Day.

"FREEDOM" rings through the fieldhouse as
the voice of Richie Havens entrances many.

MISS Emilia nostalgically converses with Cousin Limus in "The Ballad of the Sad Cafe."

LEADING War in their first number, guitarist Howard Scott really gets it on in his solo.

Spring of '72 Mom's Day and Campus Carnival

SMILING faces of clowns are common when Bradley University sets up Campus Carnival. Mike Svoboda and Ray King add their faces to the day's activities and fun.

PANFRA sing highlights activities for Mom's Day as Sigma Delta Tau and Sigma Chi show in their performance on stage.

CAMPUS Carnival, including Greeks and other independent organizations, send the fieldhouse into fun loving chaos. As a non-profit activity, Campus Carnival proceeds are donated to various Peoria area charities.

FIELDHOUSE activities on Mom's Day included a Pi Kappa Alpha-Chi Omega skit.

MORE than 700 seniors form the processional line to receive degrees
along with two honorary degrees awarded to two Peoria residents.

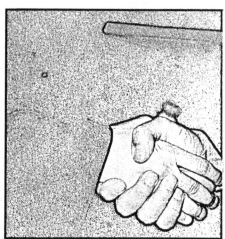

Spring '72 graduation for 700 seniors marks 75th exercises

CONGRATULATIONS go hand in hand with receiving diplomas after listening to the vice president of Hebrew University of Jerusalem.

PRECEDING graduation exercises, Dr. George Ferguson, Vice President of Academic Affairs, aids a colleague in adjusting his robe. The style of academic robes dates back to the thirteenth century.

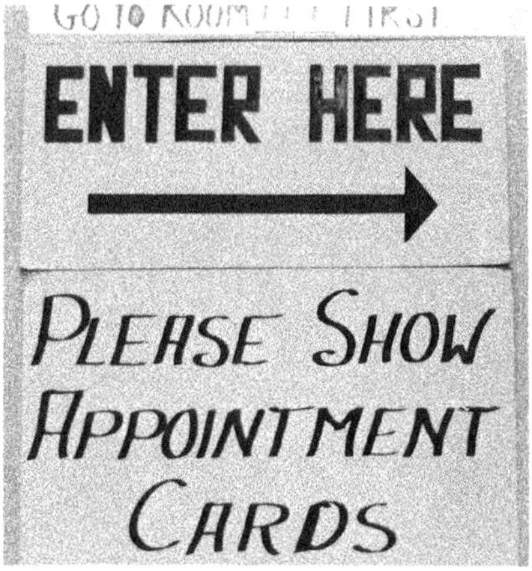

GO TO ROOM ... FIRST

ENTER HERE

→

PLEASE SHOW APPOINTMENT CARDS

EVERYONE STOP HERE

→   →

→

EVERYONE MUST STOP IN ROOM 202

→

UPSTAIRS

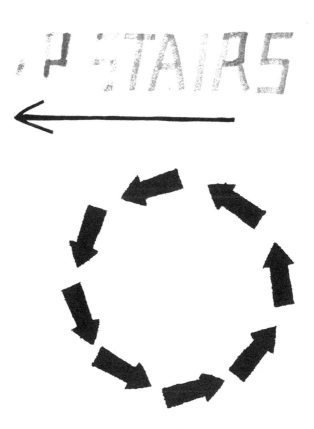

SLASHING another class, the mighty marker
takes with it the hopes of many helpless
students of getting into the class they want.
Students described the lines as the worst ever.

Registration: !#*?$$$$$*%#*!

I.D. card waiting took
up most of students'
time at Activities Fair.

STUDENTS wait for I.D. pictures to be taken after finishing registration in Bradley Hall. For the second year classes started at the end of August and finished in December for first semester.

FINALLY registration is over! What a hassle!

JAY centers and shapes another masterpiece.

OUTDOOR classes create a relaxed atmosphere.

Classes held in different environments

BIOLOGY and botany classes experiment with the plants in the environmental dome.

YAWNING and chin leaning, signs of class fatigue.

NATURE can distract a person from academic duties.

MEMBERS of the play casts know how much time rehearsals for productions take from studies.

Study—What's that???

CONCENTRATION is the name of the game as Helen Camasto prepares to catch a fast approaching egg. Other games included a tug-of-war and a pig catching contest.

SDT sorority celebrates after winning the egg tossing contest. Greek games were held in the fall this year instead of the spring months.

Greek Week Games

BANANAS proved to be a favorite among contestants of the banana eating contest during "It's the Real Greek" games.

WITH empty glass still raised, Phi Tau Gary Jones, the fraternity chug winner, proves "it's good to the last drop."

*'All greased up
and ready to kick ass'*

*"TEEN Angel" brings nostalgia to the audience
at the year's first concert, Sept. 22.*

ROCK and roll is revived as ShaNaNa
heats the Bradley Fieldhouse.

AFTER a warm up performance by Wilderness
Road, ShaNaNa comes back with four encores.

"MOTHER of Women's Lib" and author of **The Feminine Mystique,** Betty Friedan speaks to a class the night after talking in the fieldhouse for Lecture Arts.

ONE-TIME Democratic vice-presidential candidate, Senator Thomas Eagleton, spoke here to begin the Student Senate Public Relations Week in October.

Views on Women's Lib, politics, and the environment presented by prominent speakers

ADMINISTRATOR of the Environmental Protection Agency, William Ruckelshaus, discusses pollution problems and solutions during Senate PR Week.

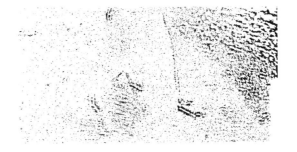

Lack of feedback ousts Fall Event

Bradley Scout, October 13, 1972, p. 6 — The elimination of the fall event this year is "due entirely to lack of student feedback," according to Bobbie Applegate, Student Center program director.

Last year's carnival was barely able to break even and the all-nighter registered a loss of about $800, Applegate said.

"The purpose of the fall event was to fill the void of homecoming being moved from the fall to midwinter which was, in turn, due to the cancellation of football," Applegate said.

"We had hoped to break even and since activities are supposedly subsidized with university tuition, we felt obliged to promote it even if we had doubts about it being a financial success."

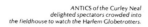
BOSTON blocks a shot against the Globetrotters during
their performance on Saturday evening, October 14.
Former Bradley star, Bobby Joe Mason plays for the team.

ANTICS of the Curley Neal
delighted spectators crowded into
the fieldhouse to watch the Harlem Globetrotters.

Globetrotter tricks thrill audience

BASKETBALL can be fun whether one is a Globetrotter or not. The new basketball court behind the bookstore provided recreation for all who enjoyed playing.

INTRAMURAL teams from each dorm floor participate in three divisions for top positions in the league.

Music and politics at the fieldhouse

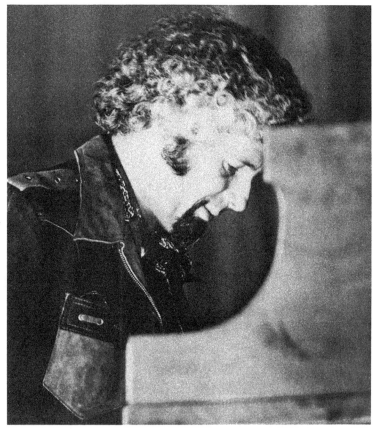

DAD'S Day performer, Peter Nero, displays the technique which has made him famous in U.S. About 3,000 people attended the concert.

FEATURED speaker at the Young Republicans' Rally, Ronald Reagan, speaks about the party campaigns.

ART work of tissue paper red, white, and blue roses epitomizes the patriotism and fanfare of the rally.

Culture on Campus

"LITERATURE and Us" is the theme of the oral interpretations
of the Wordmasters from Georgetown College. The group gave
two performances using their concept of speaking with the body.

ORIGINAL works of poetry are presented by Anselm Hollo during
the week of the Festival of Arts from October 23-27.

GAZING up at mother witch Martacloy, Pegora realizes her mother's wishes should be granted with no questions asked and leaves to capture the seven beautiful daughters at the court of King August and his wife, Queen June.

CONCENTRATION is a necessity for Greg Goyen to benefit from a practice lesson taught by Stefan Bardas, a guest pianist from North Texas University. The sessions were given in front of music classes as a part of Festival Arts.

Amazing how people

Can complicate life.

Make confusion from the simplest task;

Change or perspective

Would make this appear

A pervious view of the world.

*Carpenters and
Chi-Lites in Concert*

50

*GARRETT Communiversity receives funds from the Chi-Lites concert.
The concert was sponsored by Bradley's Black Students' Alliance.*

*SISTER and brother, Karen and Richard Carpenter, perform for a packed
fieldhouse. The enthusiasm of the pair for music and performing
in concert might have been the reason for the performance's sellout.*

Accidents
do happen

Social comments through lecture and music

BLACKS must unify their interests and then together gain the respect of those people who can bring about change. For Ron Daniels, this is the formula for successful equality.

"WE'RE all equal under God," says Jesus-rock singer Larry Norman. For him, love of each other and love of Jesus could bring us answers to many of our social problems.

INSTRUMENTALIST Bob Thomas strums a
light accompaniment for a Christmas carol.

FOR dessert a steaming hot bowl of
fiery pudding is served from the brass cauldron.

Madrigal dinner serves food and song

CANDLES blazing, the atmosphere of the fourteenth century is created by decor and costume.

Carousel presents
'Middle of the Night'

DR. Collins Bell, of the Bradley Speech and Theatre Arts, portrays a widower of 54 who falls in love with a girl 21 years younger.

CRITICISM, anger, and frustration humanize the personalities of each of the characters and they don't hold anything back.

STAGE sets, in a middle American style, create a specious but homey scene. For the limited space of the theatre, a challenge.

Ask Ann Lenders

DEAR ANN, I am a Bradley student and quite concerned about my grades. Although students say they are putting less emphasis on grades and more importance on what is really being learned, I know they still realize its the grade that counts now. This is evident by the amount of cheating which occurs during each semester. All kinds of methods are used; plagiarism, stealing homework, buying test answers, and bribing teachers. It is becoming difficult for a student, like myself, who is being compared with these students for achievement to keep the grades up. What can I do to keep up with these people who have an unfair and an illegal advantage? A BORN LOSER

DEAR BORN LOSER, *What comes to mind is the old cliche, "If you can't beat them, join them." This does seem to be the easiest way to stay with your classmates grade wise, but this motto is a cliche. As you say, it is not today's grade that is all important, but how much is really learned. So why not let yourself be concerned with learning and not grades. Do you want to get out of college with pieces of paper with lots of good "looking" A's or with a knowledge that will not fail you in the real world, that is the decision that you must make for yourself, no one can make it for you. ANN*

DEAR ANN, "We've got a deal that you won't be able to refuse!" That's what the Bradley University Bookstore says at the end of each semester when they recall the used books. When the students are lucky, they get a small refund. But most of the time students must sell books back to the "Company" and settle for twenty-five cents for a book that might have cost as much as twenty-five dollars. The paperback book is being used by many instructors because it is cheaper than the hard back edition. Since it is cheaper, the bookstore doesn't feel obligated to give even a quarter for it. Most often the student can only whisper something under his or her breath and stalk off poorer but wiser. Just knowing not to expect any credit for these expensive items doesn't help the problem of having a shelf full of useless books not connected with ones major. They can't be sold to another poor student taking the same elective or requirement because "The new edition is being used." A student could go broke paying for the books for school. What can I do until the B.U. bookstore really makes a deal I can't refuse?
ANOTHER BANKRUPT BRADLEY UNIVERSITY STUDENT

DEAR BANKRUPT, *You could stop buying books, not very practical, but thrifty. The alternatives seem to be a system through which books could be obtained by students wholesale to eliminate the bookstore as a mediator. Or a student owned bookstore could take some of the inflation out of the book market by becoming a center for students to buy and sell their books without the aid of the bookstore on campus. Of course a project like this takes the cooperation of all the students on the campus, but it seems possible. Until then, good luck getting a "good deal".
ANN*

Classified Ads

Help Wanted

Medium-size, private, Midwestern university seeks established member of silent majority to fill position of security director. Must be able to fill position that has no defined qualifications or duties. Former graduates preferred. Position available as of November thirtieth.

Equal opportunity employer needs several hundred high school graduates who would like to donate four years of their lives to serious research programs at Mid-Western university. Should be enthusiastic, idealistic, and in a search for truth. Moral of applicants will be considered, however, all applications will be accepted by employers immediately.

For Sale

Sixty-four acres of property in quiet residential area in second largest city in Ill. Many valuable facilities available for conventions, banquets, and Boy and Girl Scout Camporees: 2500 rooms with bath, spacious lawns, cafeteria services, vending machines.

The Eyes Have It!

Just for fun- and for a free toke gift for gifted guessers- can you guess the celebrity to whom these eyes belong? RULES: Winners are listed on page 427, but only if received by midnight February 30. The limit is one guess per major per yearbook which includes guessing for another major.

Don't You Hate It When

... you lock yourself out and the phone is ringing.
... you try to park your car and find a VW in the spot you thought was empty.
... there is nothing for dinner but liver and frozen hamburger.
... you start a term paper the night before it's due.
... the phone next door rings all night.
... you only have plastic silverware to cut your steak.
... someone talks about biology class while you're eating dinner.
... you sneeze in class and can't find a kleenex anywhere.
... the only thing on TV is **Second Cousin of Frankenstein meets Mob**y **Dick.**
... you realize you have stapled your paper together upside down.
... you finally get up for that 8:00 class and it has been cancelled.
... your roommate forgets you are in the shower and locks you out.
... you answer the phone and all you can hear is heavy breathing.
... all the books on reserve that you needed have already been taken out.
... you finally get your theme typed and find you have spelled your name wrong.

Famous Quotations

"It's okay to be fake if you're real about it." — George Carlin
"If you push something hard enough, it will fall over." — Fire Sign
"You're as sharp as a marble." — Don Knotts
"It goes in, it must come out." — Fire Sign
"Nothing is improbable." — Joe Doe
"Shut the door and the light stays on." — Fire Sign
"I think, therefore I am." Plato
"Soooo Hi gang, What's the Scoop?" — Barb Salins
"Give them a light and they'll follow it anywhere." — Principal Poop
"Close, but no banana." — Cecil Humbolt
"Holy Mudhead, Macherel." — Peorgie
"Decent Harold, Gravy, Swell, News, Out of state, Farm out,
and Right Arm." — Cast of Thousands
"You so smart, who won Second World War?" — General Fang
"No argument or problem is so big that it can't be run away from" —
Anonymous
"You can fool some of the students some of the time
And fool some of the students all of the time
But you can even fool all of the students all of the time." — Someone

Editorial

Everyone seems to be continually dwelling on the bad aspects of this university. This is wrong, this is wrong, this is wrong. Even throughout this publication we have tended to put down the university and speak about some of the bad aspects. Of course, every university has some bad things, and granted, Bradley has its share of problems. However, we'd like to point out some good things about this school that happened and that most of you don't know about.

Bradley has had 16 consecutive winning seasons in basketball. That's the sixth best record in the nation.

Over a quarter of this year's freshmen were in the top 10 percent of their high school classes.

Bradley has one of the highest percentages in the nation of students registered to vote.

The Senate PR Week was one of the first such events in the country and it was very successful.

Only .025 percent of this year's freshmen flunked out — the lowest ever.

There are 24 hour parietal hours in most dorms. Students are now allowed refrigerators in their dorm rooms. Freshman women no longer have hours.

Lost and Found

Lost — on or near Bradley Campus, $7200.00 in small bills. If found please contact the nearest graduating senior.

Lost — one lid, between Bradley Hall and the Varsity Theatre on Main St.

Found — one rather weathered wooden Indian. Several feathers missing, but could be repaired at great expense.

Involvement

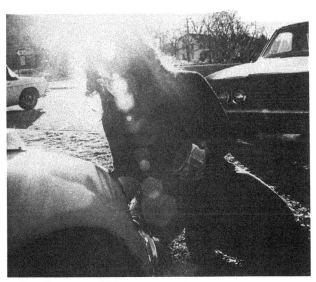

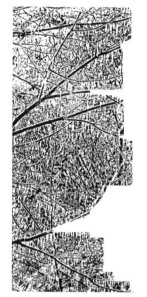

Grey mushroom puffs
Sprouted above the grounds.
They hovered for a day or two then
Gently opened fire
Pelting white bullets
On the innocent below,
Then disappeared,
In the Dark,
And the snow fell,
And the Earth froze,
And the wind calmed,
And there was silence
When the first signs of day were
Mirrored by the naked limbs of
Earth bound monsters trying to
Support their glassy cases.
They stood imprisoned by the
Cruelty of Winter's Rage.

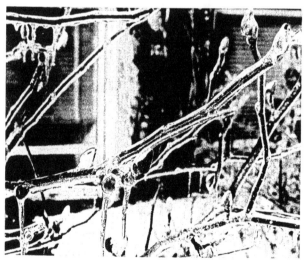

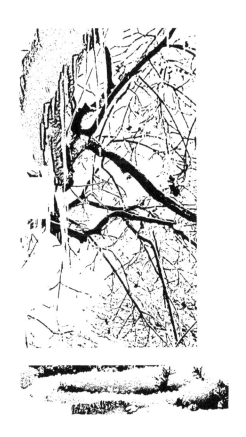

THIS young plant is only one of the many varieties of
vegetation which is grown in the domed greenhouse for
use by the biology faculty and students in experiments.

STUDENTS unwillingly hand their money to the Bradley
Bookstore each semester to pay for their books.

Tools for Study

STUDYING different slides is important for a young chemist if she is to recognize bacterial cultures in the laboratory.

ART students melt their own materials for sculpture classes. This is only one step in creating an original masterpiece.

Variety in class reactions

RESTING your head on your arm is one method of staying awake.

QUESTIONS and laughter are signs of an enthusiastic class.

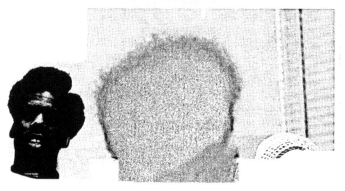

INTEREST in the subject matter can make
note taking a pleasure rather than a chore.

PROPER dissection of a frog takes a great
amount of practice and concentration.

Fieldhouse events draw sparse attendance

PASSIVENESS is growing in the U.S. We will lose our freedom if "the people" don't become aware of what goes on in Congress — the most important problem in our present political system according to Senator Birch Bayh.

TICKETS went on sale for Mason
Profitt and Steely Dan, but Steely Dan
couldn't make it. So tickets went on
sale for Mason Profitt and the
Hollies, but the Hollies couldn't make
the concert either. Finally the
program consists of Mason Profitt
and Peoria's own Dan Fogelberg.

SECRETARY of HEW Elliot Richardson, now Secretary of Defense, spoke at Founders Day on
the themes of money and the survival of private institutions.

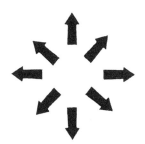

Sit silently alone.
Contemplate this
Time.
Yourself, your mind, your soul
Alone.
Untouchable, timeless
Contemplating
Yourself, your mind your soul,
Can reach out
Boundless, timeless
To touch the
World.
The self, the mind, the soul of the
Time and its
People.
All alone in contemplation.

MELLOW, earthy tunes join with poetic lyrics to produce the music of Gordon Lightfoot, homecoming's concert feature. He plays a continuous concert and sees no need to fill the time with talk, but his one comment is Bradley is the only place he has ever had the chance to hear applause in stereo.

SEVEN to seventy-seven is the score on the board, but only because the board is broken. The real score is tied at seventy-seven each. Suspense to the last seconds of the game and a freethrow by Jim Caruthers gives a homecoming victory.

Homecoming
Heros and Villians

*TRY-OUTS were held three months in advance of Carousel's last production of the year, **The Andersonville Trial.** Two other productions this year were **Four Seasons,** a love story that proves people really can't change, and **Theatre Potpourri,** a collection of comedy scenes from Shakespeare's works.*

VILLIANS are much better people to portray. A hero has to worry about getting old, and bags under the eyes; but a villian, the older he gets the better, the deeper the wrinkles the less make-up necessary. Vincent Price is quite a villinous villian, but only when acting, he claims. His humor and acting talents combined to produce a delightfully different kind of lecturer at Bradley.

Lectures and dancers add to campus culture

BRADLEY alumnus James Parks, guest speaker for the Olive B. White lecture, speaks on one of the best painters in the "Hudson River" tradition, Duncanson. Parks is himself a painter, lithographer, sculptor, art educator, and art historian at Lincoln University.

RABBI Mosha Paris discusses the role of the black Jew in his lecture sponsored by Hillel.

DANCERS and singers in color-
ful, traditional Slavic dress
present the culture of the area
through their two-hour program. The group consists of
Duquesne University students
who perform each weekend
in various parts of the country
and at the same time carry a
full study load.

Together

We joked together on the weekends.
We cheered together during the games.
We smiled together before the Mondays.
We talked together at the houses.
We walked together after the classes.
We parted together for the end.

Campus
Potpourri

REMEMBER
late nights of study at the library,
ventures in the quad,
football games in the mud and rain,
missing basketball games for night classes,
skating to class because of the ice,
short week-ends and vacation times,
and people you'll miss, both student and
faculty members who helped you get by.
All the things that make us Bradley.

competition

COMMENTARY

As basketball goes so goes Bradley. A sport that has been synonymous with the name Bradley University for as long as most people can remember. Bradley basketball has lost its spark and what is going to happen to this institution of higher learning? What does a school in a financial deficit do when it has lost its main selling point?

Although the fieldhouse still remains full at games, fans come away with a sense of disappointment and impending doom when the team loses games it should have won, when the team employs stall tactics that don't work as far as the fans are concerned, and when players have far too many "off" nights.

"Bradley basketball at its best" seems to be a dying tradition at the university. It is going the way of other traditions that have died on campus — football, homecoming, and school spirit.

Where has all the spirit gone? Granted, the rah-rah college days are gone, but what has happened to pride in one's school — that sense of nationalism localized to a specific area? Can there ever again be the phenomenon classified as school spirit here?

Perhaps it can be regenerated but it's up to students, faculty, and administrators. Together they have created the apathetic atmosphere that engulfs Bradley's every pore, that surrounds it at every entrance.

With facilities that leave much to be desired, the university tries to recruit students and keep those students already here satisfied with a glorified airplane hanger, and a promise of a new physical education facility that has been repeated for the last 10 years.

Though many find it hard to believe there are other sports at Bradley besides the "god-almighty" sport of basketball. Minor sports don't seem to be a big business for this university however. When few spectators turn out to see teams that have excellent records and are doing well this season and they get no publicity or recognition (this publication included) there is something wrong. Is it because of the conditioning students get here? All they hear is talk of basketball. Many students don't realize that there is a swim team or a wrestling team. But it could be due to the fact that most of these "minor" sports do not take place on campus because there are not adequate facilities here. Could this be the reason football died — the stadium was five miles from campus?

However, there is always hope. At the end of every bad or mediocre season the quote, "We're optimistic and looking forward to next year" can be heard, But how many next years are there going to be? How long can students go on dreaming of "Next Year"? Why not face reality!

Individually they are the netters, tankers, cagers, harriers, pucksters, etc., but collectively they are all the BRAVES!!

Bradley Basketball means

the team......

and
Coach
Joe
Stowell.

Varsity starts with 0-4 record in Valley

LOOKING *for a teammate to pass to, Seymour Reed ended the game scoring 33 against Tennessee Tech.*

Varsity Basketball FRONT ROW: Jim Perryman, Tim Altoff, Greg Smith, Seymour Reed, Sam Allen, Don Hogeboom, Gil Pacey, Mark Dohner, and Coach Joe Stowell. SECOND ROW: Coach Chuck Buescher, Tom Les, Dave Klobucher, Doug Shank, Mike Harrell, Doug Pomatto, Jim Caruthers, Jim Zimmermann, Henry Thomas, and Coach Joe Allen.

CAUGHT between two opposing players from University of Wisconsin at Green Bay, top freshman guard Jim Caruthers attempts to add two points to the score.

IN the first game of the season Mike Harrell goes up for two of his 20 points; he also garnered 12 rebounds in the contest against Wabash College.

PLAYERS must remain attentive to the game in case they become quick replacements.

THE undefeated Junior Varsity's determination proved valuable in their victory against highly rated Lincoln Junior College.

PLAYERS await the outcome of the spinning tip-off between Mark Dohner and the center from University of Wisconsin-Milwaukee.

Stowell starts youngest team in Brave's history

LEAPING high into the air, Seymour Reed tips in a missed shot against Wichita State which paved the way for the Brave's first conference victory.

FANS never see the sweat of over 20 hours practice each week which culminates in the weekend games.

Brave's first Junior Varsity team in twenty years

WITH concentration John Carroll shoots for a point.

GATHERING up a loose ball is a pleasure for Paul Zander.

WITH consistent scoring of about 30 points a game, Tim Altoff led the JV in a winning season.

Junior Varsity FRONT ROW: Marvin Bausman, Tony Calanca, Paul Zander, and Ed Miksis. BACK ROW: Coach Chuck Buescher, Roger Coulter, Carl McDonald, Randy Hamilton, John Carroll, and Mike Rucks.

Braves 'team' includes varying members

DANCING to the traditional Indian chant, the Bradley Brave arouses spirit before games.

WAVING goodbye to an opposing player who has fouled out, the crowd supports the Braves. A change in ticket policy allowed students to pick up tickets from 9 to 3 on days of games.

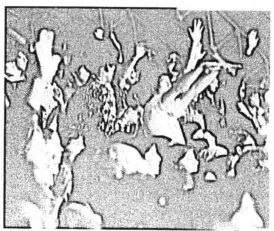

REFEREES take time out to
aid in keeping the basketball
court in shape for the team.

CHEERLEADERS express
varying emotions during one
of the Braves' games.

Golf '72

Golf Team FRONT ROW: Dave Nell, Brad Luecke, and Brent Inman. BACK ROW: Roland Edwards, Barry Mason, John Schoenheider, Rod Johnston, and Coach Jim Spink.

POSING with an iron, Barry Mason looks like a real pro for the golf team.

Tennis '72

WITH mighty force, Dana DeWindt prepares to send the ball across the court for his first serve.

SERVING the ball, a player practices at the Bradley Park courts.

PRACTICING his volleys, Dana DeWindt works on his backhand hitting.

Baseball Team FRONT ROW: Darrell Gomes, Jim Micnheimer, Joe Vespa, Gary Carter, Paul Herzog, Rick Buckner, Jack Monick, Chuck Hammond, Larry Thurston, Robert Hases, Neil Halpern, and Terry Shay. BACK ROW: Coach Leo Schrall, Dave Klobucher, Gary Bowe, Rick Burritt, Steve Welch, Jim Ferguson, Tom Stonebock, Dave Diesselhorst, Brian Rutkie, and Assistant Coach Charles Buescher.

BATTER, Dave Diesselhorst, stands up to the plate and sends the ball into the outfield.

92

Baseball '72

FINE pitching ability is shown by Jack Monick.

RELAY runner, Bruce Ulrich, speeds by with baton in hand.

Track Team FRONT ROW: Bill Hasselbacher, Gary Wallington, John Armstrong, Bruce Ulrich, Wayne Tumminello, Carol Coram, Dave Neal, Mel Diab, Phil Gamache, and Rick Kennedy. SECOND ROW: Mike Libbee, Jim Potter, Mark Brewer, Kim Brokaw, Larry Grant, Courtney Todd, Larry Butler, Jerry McMahon, Jim Winfield, Marc Jones, and Steve Wright. BACK ROW: Bob Cook, Tom Bueschel, Jerry Rose, Steve Ivey, Bob Kingery, Marty Conway, Randy Crady, Bob Marich, and Coach John Schoof.

94

Track '72

IN the mile relay, Bob Cook passes the baton to teammate Mike Libbee for the next leg of the race against Southern Illinois University—Edwardsville.

880 runner, Bruce Ulrich finishes his exhaustive race.

Team morale high
as season ends

FINE offensive skills are shown by Vic Trinkus.

Soccer FRONT ROW: Habeeb Atesh, Jorge Bustamante, Charlie Puffer, Wes Welsh, Wally Craft, Tom Cauthen, Terry Perkins, and Ben Gasirowski. SECOND ROW: Ollie Wasyncuk, Steve Perestam, Vic Trinkus, Cal Coolidge, Don Phipps, Brad Madreperl, Mike Shrock, and Rick Watters.

BATTLING for the ball, Bob de Gomar and Ollie Wasyncuk, begin to get the jump on their opponents.

TO keep the ball from Western Illinois University, Bob de Gomar runs downfield.

Bradley site picked for Missouri Valley Conference meet

AGAINST Western Illinois, Al Smith makes his move.

WHILE timers watch, two Bradley harriers — John Sorocco and Doug Nichols — press on toward the end.

Cross Country Team FRONT ROW: Jeff Wright, Bob Marich, Tom Campbell, Rick Smathers, John Sorocco, and John Leonard. BACK ROW: Mel Diab, John Armstrong, Jim Winfield, Doug Nichols, Al Smith, Carl Iserman, Tony Brocatto, and Bill Patterson.

Skating Braves get Indoor Rink

Hockey FRONT ROW: Bob Naumann, Bob Spitz, Doug Mitsuoka, Mark Eveland, Bruce Nelson, Dan Fergus, and Mike Knize. SECOND ROW: Mike Romano, Coach Pete Bardezbanian, Craig Curry, Darren Gerry, Tom Lind, Paul Curran, Lee Montgomery, Greg Adams, Phil Adamski, Roger Ruthhart, Mark Worely, and Assistant Coach John Thorp.

PLAYING twelve games in the month of February kept the Bradley icemen at a hurried pace.

MASTERFUL stick handling by Lee Montgomery keeps the puck away from Marquette.

A shot — and hopefully a goal by Mark Worely.

FOR the first time in four years, crowds are able to cheer on their favorite players indoors.

IN their first year, the Wrestling Club tried to activate another sports interest on campus.

Wrestling Club FRONT ROW: Pat McGinnis, Jim Ryan, Randy Bobus, Wayne Marx, and Jim Santostefano. SECOND ROW: Chuck Nelson, Phil Moores, John Fabecich, and Jim Stauner.

Wrestlers debut; Tankers spend time on road

IN a triangle meet against Millikin and Wheaton, diving excellence was exhibited. Trying to come back after an excellent season last year, the team was hampered due to the loss of graduating seniors.

PRACTICING before a meet, a swimmer uses a kickboard to work on his leg strokes.

VARSITY BASKETBALL

BU		
92	Wabash	75
38	U.C.L.A.	73
72	Wisc.-Milwaukee	74
72	Western Ill.	63
100	Tennessee Tech.	83
108	Emporia State	77
108	Northeast La.	76
76	Cincinnati	83
79	St. Bonaventure	77
73	Tulsa	82
74	Memphis State	76
101	West Texas State	104
59	New Mexico State	63
86	Wichita State	82
87	North Texas State	74
66	Wisc.-Green Bay	60
59	Drake	70
74	Louisville	91
64	Memphis State	79
86	St. Louis	69
73	Iowa State	90
65	Wichita State	73
78	Louisville	84
99	Valdosta State	66
89	Drake	88
71	St. Louis	85

WITH great ease, Sharon Biolchin dribbles her ball downcourt.

FOOTBALL, basketball, volleyball, gymnastics, and swimming are some of the wide variety of sports open to women.

Women's sports offer
competition with other schools

CHEERLEADERS, the pride and spirit behind our teams, must first make it past tryouts.

WOMEN were never meant to play football, but they are often more exciting than the men.

Sports play major part in lives of fraternity men

CHEERING on their brothers and friends, Bradley Park became the place on weekend afternoons.

ON fall afternoons Greeks become football carrying jocks. Looking for a receiver a Phi Kapp Tau quarterback tries to avoid the rush.

CROWDS jam Hewitt to watch wrestling championships and back favorites with "house spirit."

NOT only wrestling but Greeks participate in football, basketball, softball, volleyball, golf, and tennis throughout the year to try to capture the all-sports trophy for their house.

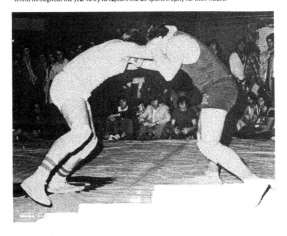

BATTLING in the semifinals for the championship, Sigma Nu takes on Theta Chi. However, the Theta Xi's ended up winning the fraternity football title.

Leagues include many sports

TRYING to beat ISA, the Vets attempt two points. Teams in the Independent League included AKPsi, APO, ISA, ROTC, SΦD, and Vets.

DORM football teams play their games on weekday afternoons in the quad.

PASSING to a teammate, John Swidergal of APO hopes to beat AKPsi. Basketball, football, and softball comprised sports for the Independent League.

110

TWO-HANDED tags stop players in league rules. Independent League played their games on weekends in Bradley Park.

MUD ball in the quad became a popular sport among each dorm floor's team members.

Bowling Team

TRYING for their seventh straight conference championship, a bowler looks for a strike.

Men's Bowling Team FRONT ROW: Steve Butler, Jim Warda, and Neal Kaufman. SEC- OND ROW: Chuck Goldberg, Arv Hansen, George Kontos, Rex Bell, Gary Smith, Gary Pon, and Bill Gaston. BACK ROW: Greg Kaufman, Ed Shavitz, Gary Understein, and Ed

Peters. Girls' Bowling Team FRONT ROW: Mary Jo Sobieraj and Denise Adams. SECOND ROW: Laura Chase, Ann Marie Glecier, and Robin Lazarus. THIRD ROW: Marie Slawniak and Nancy Somers. BACK ROW: Chris Johnson and Jaki Gardner.

habitations

COMMENTARY

If the dorm doesn't rip you off, your landlord will, and how about getting ripped off by 40 guys for brotherhood?? Yes, each type of habitation at Bradley has its own individual rip-off and how can we ever escape it?

Dorms — Living in the dorms seems to be one endless waiting line. Wait for the elevator, wait for a washing machine, wait for a free shower stall. Wait in line to eat breakfast, lunch, dinner, for food you can barely get down at times.

Two to a room, 40 to 80 to a floor, several hundred to a dorm — an assortment of experience. Despite the cell-type living, the poor food, the paper thin walls, dorm living went on undisturbed. A growing apathy concerning fellow floormates and activities that the dorm tried to sponsor such as the coffeehouse, persisted in the dorms.

Apartments — At last a place to sit that isn't a desk or a bed. Living off-campus is a consumer education in itself. Learning where the least rip-off grocery store is to shop for food; that Convenient isn't that convenient price-wise or good food-wise.

Take advantage of your landlord before he takes advantage of you. Learning that where you are living really isn't worth the rent you are paying but that there is nothing you can do if you want to be half-way close to campus. Besides there's nowhere to move because everyone else has the same problem.

There's the promises of keeping in touch with friends but the reality of the apathy that comes with not being right on campus and it's so much easier to not go out of your way but back to "your place."

Greeks — The decision to "Go Greek" because you meet more people together or for whatever reason. Are you sacrificing your individuality? Most Greeks say no but isn't every fraternity and sorority typed by those not in it? We've all heard that ChiO's are this type and Theta Xi's are all that way.

What's it all about — those names with Xs, upside down V's and triangles? Do Greeks know what it's all about?

Can Greeks claim to know the real meaning of the words unity, brotherhood, and sisterhood?

Commuters — At last an ideal lifestyle! No landlords — no roommates — no cafeteria lines. But there can be hassles with parents. Where is there a place to rest between classes? Where is there a place to close off or let the world in?

Trying to find a parking place is getting worse every day. "You can't even leave campus in the middle of the day 'cause you won't be able to park anywhere when you get back," said one student. Of course nothing is being done about it and no one is trying to get anyone to do anything about it. Life just goes on.

CAFETERIA food service came under scrutiny this year with food surveys taken by Senate and meetings with Canteen Food Service to improve the quality of the food.

LUNCH time at the dorms consists of waiting in line for cafeteria serving and then hunting for a free table.

Dorm living facilities

LAUNDRY rooms on each floor or the basement of each dorm provide chances for residents to wash their clothes.

DORM rooms may be used for many activities, one of which may be studying. Rooms are cells for residents that can be turned into fantastic facilities with a little imagination and money.

Relaxing in the dorm

COMIC books help students to relax after
a hard day of classes and studying.

TACKLING a friend eases frustrations.

LOUNGES are good places for taking it easy, watching TV, or meeting someone special.

GETTING pimped, (a tradition on campus) a student is assaulted by shaving cream.

RAPPING with friends continues to be a favorite pastime.

Residents should be prepared to wait . . . and wait . . . and wait — FOR FOOD,

FOR MAIL,

FOR ELEVATORS.

Sometimes it's worth the waiting . . .

and sometimes it isn't.

Leisure time in the

As exciting as dorm life is, residents still have leisure time for —
CARD GAMES,

NEEDLEWORK.

WRITING LETTERS,

dorms

and a little EXERCISE.

STUDYING (but only when absolutely necessary).

TELEPHONE service, an integral part of dorm life, became a part of each room this year.

SOME residents complain of having strange roommates but this is often over-exaggerated.

AS maid service is no longer provided for private rooms, things accumulate quickly

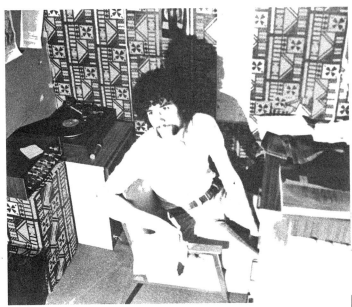

RESIDENTS can decorate their rooms in any way, as long as it's removable; one idea is moving furniture, another is wallpapering.

Dorm sponsors activities

STUDENT entertainment, popcorn, and peanuts — fare at first semester's Coffee House in Williams Hall's west cafeteria.

COFFEE house opened and closed at the end of the semester due to lack of student interest. It reopened second semester as Goldin's Grill.

CASINO Night turned cafeterias into gambling establishments for an evening.

DORM sponsored Casino Night brings many students to try their hand with luck.

ROOMS may take on many forms as each resident makes the room uniquely his.

Co-ed living, parietal hours update dorms

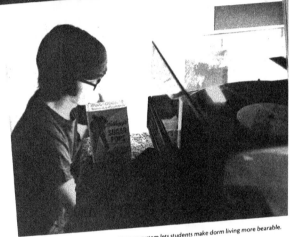

STUDYING to music on a "great" stereo system lets students make dorm living more bearable.

SLEEP — at times many students
wonder exactly what it means.

DORM residents gather in the hall for a rap
session. Twenty-four hour parietal hours
enabled residents to visit with the opposite sex
any time that they wished.

UNIQUE furnishing adorn many students' apartments such as this coffee table.

UNIQUE furnishing adorn many students' apartments such as this coffee table.

OFF-CAMPUS residents find a place to study that's not a desk or a bed.

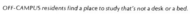

Off-campus life presents new living situations

COOKING is one of the many advantages to living in an apartment. Junior women were allowed off-campus for the first time due to a new ruling requiring all freshmen and sophomores to live in dorms and any junior or senior to live off-campus, if they want to.

WHEN the refrigerator looks bare . . . .

off-campus students know it's time to go shopping at A&P WEO, K Mart, or Thomson's.

DISHES tend to pile up in the sinks of apartment dwellers for days on end until someone needs a glass and then the dishes get done.

CLEANING an apartment can be a job that you never want to start Sandy Ascot discovers as she ponders where to start.

Household duties of off-campus life

WALKING a dog becomes part of off-campus living since most landlords allow pets and the Bradley dorms don't.

LAUNDROMATS are a necessity for many apartment dwellers since they don't have machines available like dorm residents do.

Off-campus relaxation comes in many forms

FRIENDS enjoy partying at apartments off-campus like Gaslight or Timberbrook.

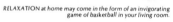

RELAXATION at home may come in the form of an invigorating
game of basketball in your living room.

GETTING together for parties with plenty of space is one of the
advantages of off-campus living compared to the dorms.

PETS add to relaxation in off-campus housing.

JUST having a cold beer in his kitchen is relaxing for Dan Harmon.

Campus homes for commuters

Homes on campus for students who commute may be the Student Center Lounge . . . . .

the parking lot . . . . . .

the library. . . . .

or the Sit'n'Bull room.

The 'other side'
of Greek life

PCFA

AT formal calling out PCFA executive secretary Roy Berg congratulates a new pledge.

PCFA Jim Steiner, Dave Stephenson, Dan Ball, Mike Strauss, and Ron Mixer.

Panhellenic Council, the governing body for the eight social sororities on campus helped to sponsor the annual blood drive. They also helped with formal rush for houses, and oversaw sorority functions.

In an effort to be more responsive to fraternity problems the Interfraternity Council reorganized into the President's Council for Fraternity Affairs. Each president of the fraternitites became members of the governing body. Among PCFA's activities for the year were the annual blood drive, a state-wide canned food drive, and repainting of the bleachers at Meinen Field.

Panhellenic Council

Panhellenic Council FRONT ROW: Roseanne Schloss, Sheryl Solomon, Francis Cook, Jackie Duda, and Linda Chamness. SECOND ROW: Jackie Ripka, Cathy Cox, Amy Meth, Sue Moore, Cindy Siokos, Nadine Liber, and Sue Reihansperger.

Alpha Epsilon Phi

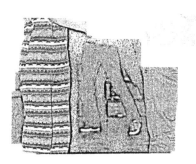

AN AE Φ smile is in order at
the Mom's Day Pan-Fra Sing.

ANOTHER banana for Diane Ohsman
at the Banana Eating Contest
where AE won second place.

1. Ellen Touretz
2. Cheryl Blumenthal
3. Marilyn Boleman
4. Sally Levy
5. Suey Cypkin
6. Jan Hall
7. Susie Kopel
8. Carole Hermele
9. Gloria Friedman
10. Monica Avery
11. Roseanne Schloss
12. Dee Dee Davis
13. Gail Stewart
14. Sheryl Solomon
15. Barb Frackman
16. Jody Wallens
17. Diane Ohsman
18. Lonnie Glass
19. Holly Edelman
20. Wendy Printz

1. Wayne Levy
2. Peter Rubenstein
3. Terry Poulliard
4. Jon Gurkoff
5. Jeff Small
6. Richie Kamp
7. Mike Hollywood
8. Denny Goodman
9. Steve Tick
10. Mike Strauss
11. Al Rappaport
12. Bob Karm
13. Eddie Duesette
14. Marshal Kettering

15. Frank Netti
16. Howard Averbach
17. Steve Bernstein
18. Andy Goldstein
19. Phil Wathall
20. Leo Cala
21. Bruce Magdule
22. Barry Raymond
23. Mark Gindlin
24. Scott Knaack
25. Mitchell Rappaport
26. David Elias
27. Paul Avsebel
28. Kevin Berger

29. Gary Selwyn
30. Neil Beim
31. Joe Guzoufski
32. Barry Goldman
33. Mark Fox
34. David Nuefeldt
35. Paul Sherman
36. Rick Andrulis
37. Allen Schulman
38. William F. Hollywood
39. Ira Van Leer
40. Jim Borenstein
41. John Spitznas
42. John Stuebing

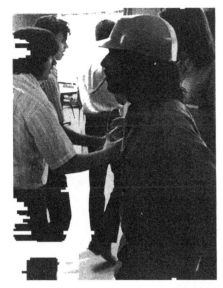

Alpha
Epsilon
Pi

RUSH parties during registration take place at each frat as members look over freshmen for prospective pledges.

RELAXING before finals start AEPi members take time out to read newspapers and magazines in a study room of a brother.

Alpha Kappa Alpha

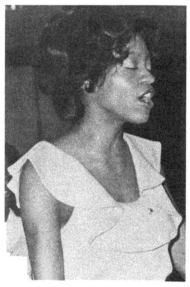

SINGING at Greek Scene an AKA performs in the all black activity.

144

AKAs perform during Greek Scene sponsored by all black fraternities and sororities on campus.

145

PLAYING in the Independent League AKPsi tries to defeat APO.
AKPsi captured first place in football at the beginning of the semester.

Alpha Kappa

1. Wayne Schupp
2. Gerry Pfeiffer
3. Brent Inman
4. Bill Gould
5. Glenn Baldwin
6. Tom "Pal" Nelson
7. Frank Poczatek
8. Tom Bicknell

ONE of the business fraternity's activities included a car wash at Sheridan Village.

Psi

9. John Warner
10. Kevin Bielik
12. Jim Connolly
13. Tom Gunyan
14. Ben Kelley
15. Bo Delong
16. Jim Moore
17. Chris Brennan

1. Joanie Niemeier
2. Liz Venturin
3. Cathy Sabin
4. Candy Gerber
5. Joan Koch
6. Kathy Jetter
7. Sheree Gollay
8. Carole Konsler
9. Ursula Kobald
10. Nancy Kistler
11. Maggy Jost
12. Peggy Young
13. Gail Samos
14. Monnie Keane
15. Karen Lackinger
16. Kathy Luscher
17. Helen Camasto
18. Terri Esrig
19. Patty McClane
20. Mary Beth Westcott
21. Susie Leeker
22. Nadine Liber
23. Lynne Salvatori

24. Lynn Wallin
25. Jeanine Schmidt
26. Terry Bush
27. Sue Hardine
28. Mary Morck
29. Kathy Biskind
30. Kathy Stiening
31. Deb Keeley
32. Andi Tun
33. Gail Magill
34. Laura Chappelow
35. Jan Mikan
36. Marilyn Janicki
37. Karen Romine
38. Candy DeGraf
39. Cathy Cox
40. Beth Elwood
41. Mary Gower
42. Mary Record
43. Sharon Kulick
44. Lynn Castles
45. Marsha Tedford

Chi Omega

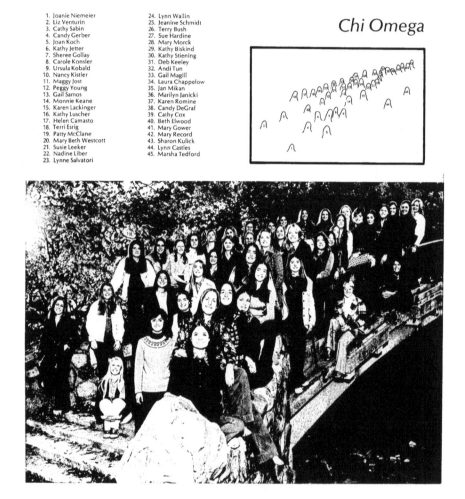

PROVING she's tops, Ursula Kobald downs her beer to win first place in the chugging contest.

RELAY race runner Lynn Castles dashes for the finish line.

1. "Dirty Ed" Bowman
2. Ray Menard
3. Frank Parks
4. Lyle Sajewich
5. "Chunky" Fazio
6. Tony Barajas
7. Ronnie Lofchie
8. Rob "Bomber" Bach
9. John "Bear" Higgins
10. Marty Smith
11. Jerry Schalk
12. Chris Peirson
13. Artie Strouss
14. Louie Reiner
15. Tony Fasano
16. Barry Bilder
17. Bill Snider
18. Al Solari
19. Brian Abrams
20. Kevin Porter

21. Dave Danielson
22. Tim Penrod
23. Steve Rugg
24. Steve Pfeiffer
25. Rick Soukup
26. Billy Bittner
27. Tom Hillmann
28. Mark Eveland
29. George Jayne
30. Roy King
31. Mark Kotlick
32. Bob "Kong" Kingery
33. Arnie Tropper
34. Tom Stelzner
35. Rob Dodds
36. Wade Walden
37. Tommy Cauthen
38. Rob Dixon
39. Denny Meyers
40. Cliff Strom

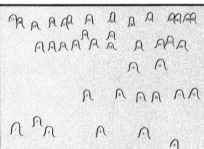

Delta Upsilon

CATCHING a greased pig wasn't too big
a challenge for Chuck Sharp at Greek Games.

FRATERNITIES enjoyed raising
money for charity at campus carnival.

1. Bev Nash
2. Ann Gysin
3. Mardona Thornton
4. Debbie Brayton
5. Cindy Posley
6. Linda Swett
7. Linda Paul
8. Carol Belback
9. Sharon Rosenblum
10. Sue Pulte
11. Mary Head
12. Barb Bergman
13. Darilyn Caskey
14. Debbie Stein
15. Martha Mehrings
16. Carolyn Young
17. LeeAnn Kozak
18. Helen Czachorski
19. Linda Chamness
20. Sue Woods

Delta Zeta

GULPING down a banana Bev Nash tries to place first.

CLOWNS Linda Swett and Linda Chamness add to festivities at Campus Carnival.

BEFORE dinner Gamma Phi's gather in the
living room to rap about the day.

Gamma
Phi
Beta

SINCE Christmas presents are piled under the tree, Amyre Coleman adds hers.

1. Marcy Goodman
2. Sheila Stiles
3. Kathy Arkwell
4. Denise Farina
5. Mary Jo Smith
6. Bev Rautenberg
7. Janet Smith
8. Cheryl Kolator
9. Barb Hanekamp
10. Amyre Coleman
11. Terrie Dangler
12. Pam Pidcoe
13. Camille Petriska
14. Sharon Biolchin
15. Joan Myers
16. Chris Sweeney
17. Jacie Levy
18. Sandy Reimer
19. Madeline Mitchell
20. Lynn Olsen
21. Susie Moore

22. Melissa Byers
23. Kathy Kriessl
24. Holly Lang
25. Betsy Althoff
26. Corky Pfiester
27. Dyan Scherr
28. Mary McClane
29. Jane Richards
30. Louise Boston
31. Melissa Sauter
32. Aileen Anderson
33. Meryl Granic
34. Anne Ciambrone
35. Sally Young
36. Helaine Kane
37. Pam Witzke
38. Joanne Lynch
39. Val Green
40. Susie Fritsch
41. Bonnie Raymond

155

Lambda Chi Alpha

LCA's discuss strategy for the next down.

1. Dan Sanders
2. Tom Fillip
3. John Nagy
4. Edward Van Meyer
5. Tom Paulsen
6. Steve Orloff
7. Bob McMahon
8. Tom Chernak
9. Rich Ramello
10. Dave Long
11. Randy Rhodes
12. Jack Meyer
13. Jack Collins
14. Brad Randall
15. Andy Stefo
16. Rich Christensen
17. Bob Wicke
18. Ken Siok
19. Tony Tomaso
20. Terry Locke
21. Jeff Alexander
22. Jeff Trzaska
23. Russ O'Connor
24. John Schadl
25. John Nelson
26. Kevin Carroll
27. Phil Pritzker
28. Connie Mueller
29. Don Johnson
30. Russ Troc
31. Bob Kamerlander
32. Dave Hardy
33. Orren Pickell
34. Steve Welch
35. Doug Mitchell
36. Steve Chadesh
37. Vince Hanlon
38. Terry Wallace
39. Bruce Blumer
40. Jack Croc

CONCERN is reflected on
the faces of LCA spectators.

CONTESTANTS and their stuffed
friends visit during Lambda
Chi's Pajama Queen competition.

COUPLES enjoy the music and atmosphere at Pi Beta Phi's Winter Formal.

GULPING down the last bite of banana, Barb Taylor attempts to beat her opponent in race during Greek Week games.

Pi Beta Phi

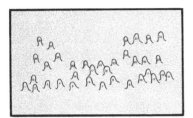

1. Laura Judd
2. Lesley Hooks
3. Dru Pardieck
4. Barb Green
5. Noel Tousey
6. Ellen Flynn
7. Carol King
8. Robyn Vaughan
9. Nancy Williams
10. Diana Evans
11. Annette Eckert
12. Judy Gora
13. Lynda Gill
14. Jamie Jarrett
15. Eva Conroy
16. Judy Stephens
17. Sue Reihansperger
18. Mary Thomas
19. Yvonne Marquart
20. Jill Alexander
21. Jane McCahill
22. Joann Churchill
23. Robyn Leslie
24. Frankie Krivohlavek
25. Mary McIntosh
26. Diane Bibbs
27. Kathy Pennington
28. Sara Bonde
29. Holly Bulter
30. Barb Taylor
31. Gillian McLaren
32. Jeanne Cunningham
33. Cherie Berndt
34. Nancy Ritter
35. Amanda Horton

STRUGGLING against his Theta Xi opponent, Dave Stieglity tries to reverse the hold and win points during the fraternity wrestling matches held in Hewitt.

LISTENING carefully, Kevin Tucker hears about the Pikes during a rush party.

GETTING lavaliered, pinned, or engaged means getting treed in fraternity life.

Pi Kappa Alpha

1. Dominic Calgi
2. Mark Galioto
3. Ronald Pope
4. Thomas Moore
5. Art Laine
6. Richard Pfister
7. Don Wittmus
8. Ken Logston
9. Brent Taylor
10. Ed Mattheeussen
11. Larry Cianforgna
12. Roger Clayton
13. Steve Ratay
14. Thomas Digate
15. Thomas Hood
16. Robert Rucker
17. Ross Timmons
18. James Long
19. James Maratea
20. Edward Welsh
21. Richard Hathaway
22. Robert Schulz
23. John Bailey
24. Robert DeHoff
25. William O'Leary
26. Chris Gooding
27. Kevin Tucker
28. Chuck Shepler
29. Jeffery Annis
30. John Lesaganich
31. David Sharp
32. Kent Sayers

1. Dan Dahlke
2. Fred Mayer
3. Dave Pletz
4. Stu Borden
5. T. Wires Dodd
6. Cris Karmis
7. Ron Mixer
8. Ron Teichert
9. Bob Solger
10. Chuck Dolan
11. Gary Kleinschmidt
12. Joe Stowell
13. Sandy Black

14. Steve Rider
15. Bob Jelen
16. Jim Mendler
17. Dave Austin
18. John Milano
19. Jeff Morris
20. Mike Vogl
21. Bill Goodwin
22. Matt Berg
23. Rush Wilt
24. Rick Mellor
25. Roger Oulette
26. Steve Corich

Sigma Alpha Epsilon

BOTTOMS up for Sandy Black at the "Real Greek" chugging contest.

MARATHON runner Joe Stowell makes his move during Greek games to finish first.

DERBY Day weekend activities
includes the traditional hussle of
painting girls shorts.

PANFRA sing pairs Sigma Chi with SDT Sorority for their skit at Mom's Day

Sigma Chi

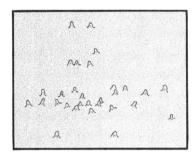

1. John Stewart
2. Doug MacNamara
3. Mike Foster
4. Greg Prullage
5. Paul Royer
6. Bob Stephano
7. Tom Bueschel
8. Greg MacMinn
9. Ed Ripka
10. Steve Wright
11. Phil Bailey
12. Bruce Buck
13. Pat McGinnis
14. Geoff Hance
15. Mark Sandell
16. Rich Buchanan
17. Dave Schlott
18. Mark Gisoudi
19. Sheldon Rosen
20. Bob Hoerner
21. Carl Shub
22. Craig Ockerlund
23. Greg Zahner
24. John Bermingham
25. Brad Friestedt
26. Larry Potempa
27. Mike Hearn
28. John Sinclair
29. Rick Scardino
30. Jim Sartori

Sigma Delta Tau

BANANAS are their favorite because they have appeal. SDT came in 1st in the banana eating contest of Greek week.

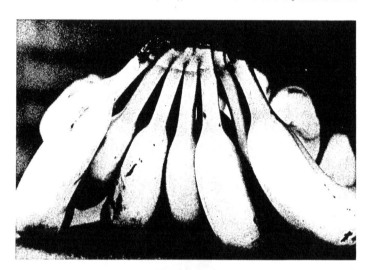

HEADING for the home stretch a relay runner puts on the speed to try to catch up.

SDT girls discuss strategies of how to catch an egg before winning the event in the quad.

1. Wendy Kanefield
2. Judi Ross
3. Shari Blumenfeld
4. Elayne Gold
5. Marilyn Zolla
6. Julie Bernstein
7. Laynie Ginsburg
8. Ruth Glazier
9. Daria Brown
10. Amy Novack
11. Amy Meth
12. Cathy Tivol
13. Lesley Hyman
14. Bonnie Katz
15. Daryl Glick
16. Sandy Lustig
17. Sandi Weiss
18. Alice Roshkind
19. Paula Gottlieb
20. Pam Greenberg
21. Mary Ellen Sheinbein
22. Debbie Cohen
23. Tobye Goldstein
24. Beth Zelden
25. Roberta Montalto
26. Sandee Wolpin
27. Wendi Freedman
28. Randey Foss
29. Lesley Linn
30. Franci Cook
31. Roni Rabins

CAR wash time took up Sigma Kappa's extra time on a Saturday morning.

CAPTURING second place in the near-beer chugging contest, Laurie MacDougall drains her glass during Greek Week.

168

1. Nancy Knowles
2. Ginny Trent
3. Sue Koukel
4. Kathy McDaniels
5. Rorie Luther
6. Marsha Caulson
7. Beth Fuchs
8. Melanie Siedlinski
9. Cindy Siokos
10. Diane Jordt
11. Berta Hostetler
12. Ruth Neumann
13. Cindy Carlson
14. Jackie Duda
15. Carol Gerhardt
16. Peggy Paetsch
17. Renee Belanger
18. Aunt Lorrie

19. Kathy Nance
20. Jody Bennett
21. Joyce Fash
22. Cathy Mical
23. Diane Stulken
24. Laurie MacDougall
25. Sherry McClenny
26. Joan Harrell
27. Robin Gibbons
28. Debbie Dukes
29. Liz Volturno
30. Carol Burrows
31. Carolyn Johnson
32. Rae Rehr
33. Pat Blum
34. Deb Ditchman
35. Joan Van Cura
36. Debbie Greenhut

37. Cathy Edmondson
38. Mary May
39. Pam Somers
40. Jan Johnson
41. Jane Beckway
42. Karen Anderson
43. Debbie Snedeker
44. Susan Edwards
45. Debbie Chase
46. Linda Kuntzi
47. Therese Maloney
48. Rondi Bogwald
49. Janet Riegel
50. Bev Small
51. Laura Sarovich
52. Amy Milton
53. Debbie Nelson
54. Jill Cope

1. Rick Rodstrom
2. Chip Donahue
3. Dean Mades
4. Bill Carlstedt
5. Mike James
6. Ken Behr
7. Pat Baikauskas
8. Craig Harrison
9. John Kouns
10. Jeff Hughes
11. George Schmid
12. Kent Brunsman
13. Rich Nubeil
14. Billy Laird
15. Sammy Palumbo
16. Marty Ceranec
17. Jeff Graves
18. Phil Adamski
19. Doug Mitsouka
20. Bob Kolpin
21. Mike Romano
22. Andy Charles
23. James Norris
24. Bob Olson
25. Mike Taylor
26. Tom Smith
27. Neil Lubarski
28. Dan Johnson
29. Gary Blazek
30. Don Kawolski
31. Jim Schneff
32. Jim Yoshinaga
33. Bob Carlstedt
34. Bill Hoare
35. George Jasinski
36. David Rasmussen
37. Tod Altoff

HALLOWEEN Party first prize winner, Mike Norris, displays his costume.

170

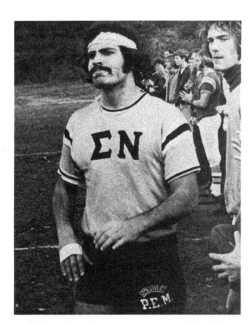

Sigma Nu

KICK one back to Pennsylvania urges Ian Malatesta.

QUARTERBACK Gary Blazek looks for a receiver.

1. Lew Leibowitz
2. John Witthuhn
3. Ron Bryze
4. Ken Maltas
5. Larry Decker
6. John Bredemeyer
7. Mike Ernt
8. Mark Teska
9. Ron Blohm
10. Guenther Hartfeil
11. Frank Pircher
12. John Young
13. Pete Reimann
14. John Kovacik
15. Craig Frommelt
16. Marty Hadank
17. Bill Peterson
18. John Henry
19. Andy Jaskierski
20. Paul Van Henkelum
21. Mike Scott
22. John Backovitch

OUT at Bradley Park Ralph Nelson runs to aid Ken Maltas stop an Alpha Kappa Psi player in Independent League football.

PRACTICING his forehand, Frank Pircher enjoys the use of the ping pong table at the engineers' fraternity.

Sigma
Phi
Delta

Tau Epsilon Phi

1. Jack (Silly) Sills
2. Bruce (Czar) Rabinowitz
3. Barry (Freak) Clark
4. Nelson (Meatball) Spiess
5. Lucien (Blaine) Clarke
6. Jimmy (Hendrix) Heinz
7. Jim (Rye Bread) Rosen
8. Mike (South) Gryll
9. Jeff (Crazy) Cole
10. Dave (Igor) Weinberg
11. Bob (Bergee) Burger
12. Beatrice Beagle
13. Mark (Baeit) Breitman
14. Dave (Cink) Perlman
15. Bob (Hawk) Taylor
16. Matt (Bait) Nardi
17. Errol (Captain Pike) Bliwas
18. Dave (Happy) Drell
19. Andy (Dragon) Drogen
20. Irving (Jock) Weinberg
21. Mike (Hockey) Karoff

22. Jim (Gone) Dwyer
23. Mark (Lunch) Lopofsky
24. Kenny (Turnoff) Tarnoff
25. Joel (Fess) Parker
26. Mark (Markie) Stuart
27. Mike (Mind) Skolnick
28. Rich (Ranger) Barnett
29. Kerry (Todi) Fields
30. Glenn (W. Sox) Smoler
31. Gerry (?) Seeger
32. Mike (Bobo) Bashkin
33. Al (Viking) Fields
34. Bob (Flower) Rose
35. Fred (Fredie) Einbinder
36. Marty (Body) Lieberman
37. Gary (Gomer) Roesenbaum
38. Jeff (Schlepp) Crohn
39. Gary (Scheib) Understein
40. Neil (Pinball) Hunter
41. Aaron (Mort) Rubin
42. Jerry (ROTC) Alexander
43. Mike (Cowboy) Gale

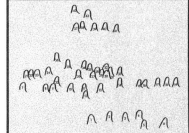

174

MOST *frat houses provide parking behind their houses and so do the TEPs.*

NEW *pledges wait to be called at formal calling out in the fieldhouse.*

Tau Kappa Epsilon

TALKING with Little Sisters makes
fraternity life more pleasant for the brothers.

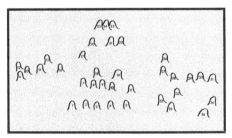

1. Dukebaum	19. Herderbaum
2. Brucebaum	20. McKeebaum
3. Davebaum	21. Hilrithbaum
4. Markbaum	22. Holmquistbaum
5. Barrybaum	23. Schefkebaum
6. Kriestnerbaum	24. Zbaum
7. Rockbaum	25. King Tuttbaum
8. Stardustbaum	26. Heinsbaum
9. Jackbaum	27. Stretchbaum
10. Gonebaum	28. Squidbaum
11. Eggertbaum	29. Squidbaum
12. Rogerbaum	30. Voightbaum
13. Toobinbaum	31. Murdanebaum
14. Porterbaum	32. Steinmanbaum
15. Glickbaum	33. Fisherbaum
16. Funderbaum	34. Larrybaum
17. Adolfbaum	35. Cedersykesbaum
18. Schwantz-	36. Chestbaum

Theta Chi

*THE tug-of-war was a muscle
tester during Greek Week.*

*THETA Chi's banner is raised
proudly at their football games.*

178

FANCY footwork and determination
prove valuable against the Sigma Nu's.

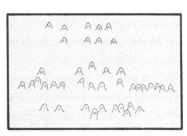

1. Frenchie
2. D
3. Mr. Suddensuit
4. Kid
5. TKE
6. Miles
7. Flea Bait
8. Norton
9. Wolf Dart
10. Scrot
11. Grease
12. Haug
13. Asoris
14. Walt
15. Carp
16. Dyke
17. Trux
18. Zips
19. Crowd
20. Coontzy
21. Dart Shaffney
22. Boot
23. Los
24. Bob
25. Boehmer
26. Moose
27. Horse
28. 'Eazy'
29. George
30. Pup
31. Coon
32. Bloomers
33. Cisco
34. Space Mouse
35. Reds
36. Owie
37. Jello City
38. James
39. U-Head
40. Buddy
41. Nobody Special

1. Gary "Hofenslaf" Gossett
2. David Stevenson
3. Daryl Buder
4. Joe Conklin
5. Bob Kaufmann
6. Speedy Weisen
7. Rick Orr
8. Bob Grotto
9. Fred Berl
10. Chris Towne
11. John Nuber
12. Kevin Duffy
13. Tom Mulvihill
14. Steve Rawlings
15. John Lazarus
16. Bill Suhr
17. Bob Cinnato
18. Chuck Nord
19. Paul Curran
20. Dave Duncan
21. Ratso
22. Bob Grabel
23. John Edgerton

CROWD watches as Theta Xi captures Fraternity Football Championship.

180

Theta Xi

ATTEMPTING to finish first, Roger Whyte struggles onward during Marathon race of Greek Week.

Kappa Alpha Psi

1. Larry Wilson
2. Fred Montgomery
3. Warren Wright, Jr.
4. Darrel Booth
5. Keith Cole
6. Cynthia Kilpatrick
7. Michael Sykes
8. Maxine Jones
9. Rhonda Trotter
10. Marla Duke
11. Harvey Middleton
12. Richard Buckner
13. Archie Weston
14. Jackie McLean
15. Melinda Jones
16. Connie Thurston
17. Sylvia Mills
18. Gale Kennebrew
19. Joanne Robinson
20. Beverly Mason

Phi Kappa Tau

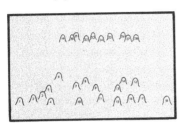

1. Al Bradshaw
2. Richard Skirball
3. Charles Frizzell
4. Ken Grisham
5. Joe Lappeglia
6. Dan Rakowski
7. Dave Isley
8. Dave Kegle
9. Keith Jones
10. Doug Schmidt
11. Michael Ritschdorf
12. Tom Skweres
13. Michael Salmi
14. Bill Vanni
15. Steve Bradley
16. Steve Telford
17. Dan Sullivan
18. John Bacilek
19. Bill Stubbits
20. Tom Rushing
21. Dan Ball
22. Gary Jones
23. John Boruch
24. John Kankis
25. Michael Knize
26. Russ Wayne
27. Gary Olson
28. Terry McGuan

Zeta Beta Tau

1. Gumpy Gordon
2. Percy Zatlin
3. Andrew Randall
4. Curls Greenfield
5. Whitey Imber
6. Zigs Bay
7. Essex Perlstein
8. Flame Lieblich
9. King Herman Yerman
10. Texas Barg

11. D. A. Strom
12. Motormouth Aletkin
13. Woody McGarrett Gollay
14. Michelle Young
15. A. J. Jablo
16. Ragman Dunst
17. Kashi Weintraub
18. Bento Weintraub
19. Ward Rubenstein
20. Charles Roblin

184

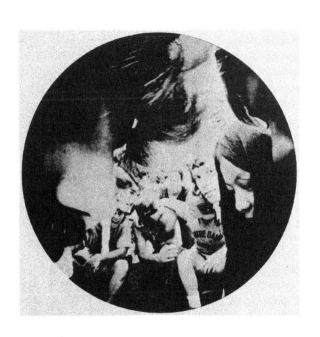

particapations

COMMENTARY

Participation, being involved, doing something worthwhile — that's what is behind the idea of organizations, groups, and clubs.

However, the apathy at this campus has also crept into its organizations, slowly but surely. An Activities Fair where 40 organizations say they want tables to be represented and then less than half of them show up, characterizes the kind of apathy taking over.

What is the idea behind organizations? Do they have a purpose if they aren't active?

Professional societies that stand for status only are out-numbering the so-called active groups on campus.

Organizations seem to exist only for students to be able to join Who's Who or add to their applications for med school, law school, or grad school that they belonged to this, this, this, AND this.

Then there's always the ultimate — the ego trip. Look at me, I'm president of this or I run that.

Participating can go on in a non-organization atmosphere, however. That is what the Student Center is for, supposedly.

How can a facility that is for the students fail in so many ways to serve the students' needs? The Student Center, built entirely with students' money, claims to serve students when it closes at 11 p.m. every night, including weekends.

There is just no place on campus that a student can go for a cup of coffee and a little rapping after 10:30. Most students don't hit the sack until 1 or later. Does serving the students mean giving them no place to go but their dorm room or apartment?

Prices at the Center for food seem to go up and up but there is no improvement in the quality of food being served.

Then there's always the Sweet Shop, paid for by the Dad's Association, which is doing good business. Students always enjoy eating. But couldn't that money have been used for better purposes when this university is in the midst of a financial deficit?

Organizing into groups can be a good force but only if people are willing to work for them to be active. The Student Center can only change by students pushing for change and that won't happen until the apathy can be eliminated on this campus.

Senate FRONT ROW: Tim *Engen,* Dan *Stieb,* Doug Dougherty, *Jeff* Hughes, and *Kim* Kelley. SECOND ROW: Neil Hunter, Jim Otten, and Steve *Wittenborn.* THIRD ROW: Pat Baikauskas, Ken *Behr,* Jacki Samuelson, John Baroni, Donna Neudecker, Lyndi *Kramer,* Jeff Serle, Mike James and Tom Orr. FOURTH ROW: Gordon Tingley, Eyde McGhee, Barb Musielak, and Dick Bardoulas. FIFTH ROW: Fish, Joyce Anthony, Rod Sumner, Nancy Serra, Barb Bergman, Darilyn Caskey, and Wayne Levy. SIXTH ROW: Bruce Anton, Kevin Tilton, Jay Krasne, and Rick Scardino.

Student Senate

Student Senate, the legislative branch of student government, kicked off their activities with a public relations week. Speakers involved in the PR campaign included Senator Eagleton of Missouri and William Ruckelshaus, director of the environmental protection agency.

Composed of 40 members, Senate planned Free University courses, a tutor program, and a test file. They also printed a student orientation booklet for incoming students, took food surveys, and tried to aid students with housing contracts.

185

The Supreme Court consists of justices, prosecutors, and a defense staff. The court rules on cases pertaining to violations of university rules. The Coffee House Committee organizes and operates the functions of the Coffee Ground Inn in Williams Hall.

Below: **Supreme Court Justices** *Annette Eckert, Dennis Holland, Chief Justice Randy Livingston, Gregory Smith, Thomas Smith, Helen Czachorski, and Gene Voss.* Bottom: **Prosecution Staff** *Gail Samos, Dan Seitz, Walter Theus, R. A. Lucas, Kerry Fields, and William Sweasy.* Right: **Defense Staff** *Don Russo, Frank Gabell, Tom Skweres, and Jean Dower.* Below Right: **Coffee House Committee** FRONT ROW: *Bob Wiebe, Michael Johnson, Carla Jones, Howard Popyer, Eyde McGhee, Richard Scott, Tom Kazunas, Ginny Beringer, and Veronica Maxey.* BACK ROW: *Wally Tuten, Turk Gryzmaca, Lynn Perez, and Carol Kearney.*

Dorm Councils helped residents solve the problems of dorm living. After officer elections, the councils began their work in the areas of food, laundry, security, and other pertinent issues. They served as a place for dorm residents to direct complaints, suggestions, and comments toward in order to improve living conditions. Together with the Interdorm Council, they helped to plan and give a Christmas party for underprivileged children of the community. Both organizations strove to coordinate activities and better relationships between residents of all dorms.

Above: **Heitz Dorm Council** FRONT ROW: Jeanette Nuckolls, Robin Gibbons, Laura McNally, Roberta Montalto, Diane Saelens, and Janet Dixon. SECOND ROW: Jan Hackel, Karen Weinstein, Marie Saul, Marybeth Genis, and Denise Wells. BACK ROW: Carrie Williams, Claire Manning, and Jackie Smith. *Above left:* **Interdorm Council** FRONT ROW: Kathy Roberts and Jackie Smith. SECOND ROW: Carla Jones, Eyde McGhee, Laura McNally, and Debbie Brenner. BACK ROW: Lynn Perez, Dan Rouse, Pat Callahan, Richard Scott, Peter Zuckerwise, and Allan Price. *Left:* **Lovelace-Sisson Dorm Council** Gregg Gaylord, Wally Tuten, Dan Caddigan, and Allan Price.

189

Above: **University Dorm Council** FRONT ROW: Cerita Brown, Lynn Perez, Carol Kearney, and Phyllis Stern. SECOND ROW: Maxine Isert, Joanne Krieberg, Dale Shapiro, Leslie Miller, Carla Jones, Debbie Apato, and Jo Ellen Guido. BACK ROW: Karen Hansen, Rita L. Pell, Debbie Block, and Kathy Roberts. *Above left:* **Geisert Dorm Council** FRONT ROW: Terri Rudolph, Mary Anne Potts, and Gwendolyn J. Hinton. BACK ROW: Dave Hruska, Dave Van Gorder, Rod Allen, Irv Weinberg, Richard Scott, Peter Zuckerwise, and Hilary LaMothe. *Far left:* **Williams Dorm Council** FRONT ROW: Michael Shannon, Eyde McGhee, Nancy Glick, Tony Lyons, Dorie Elrod, and Wendy Levy. BACK ROW: Bob Block, Don Vincz, Sandy Kalnitz, Michael Johnson, Christy Tolbert, Randy Smith, and Robyne Harrison. *Left:* **Harper-Wyckoff Dorm Council** Jim Ruckman, Win Wehrli, and Pat Callahan.

Student Center Board is designed to encourage student participation in all-school events. It plans and coordinates activities that are of general interest to the student body such as movies, concerts, and jams. Through the board's efforts, students rediscover enjoyment, leisure, and an escape from the routine of studying. Lecture Arts presents programs dealing both with important issues of the day and popular entertainment. They try to schedule events that are interesting and relevant to students at Bradley and to the Peoria community. Some of the features this year included ShaNaNa, Betty Friedan, the Carpenters, Ron Daniels, and Vincent Price.

JAMS in the ballroom include singers from many rock groups for student enjoyment.

Left: **Student Center Board** SITTING: Bruce Becker, Jack Meyer, Al Lipperini, and David Olszak. STANDING: Margaret Heckinger, Joan Myers, and Diana Hauter. *Below:* **Lecture Arts Committee** SITTING: Pam Miller, Joyce Murphy, Sue Kaldahl, Darilyn Caskey, Linda Chamness, Barb Bredel, Bev Nash, Joanne Skiba, and Linda Paul. STANDING: Rick Wargo, Mike Sklar, Tom Lebak, and Dave Pounds.

Circle K, service group connected with the Kiwanis Club of Peoria, sponsored ecology projects on campus. This year's activities included a "Take Your Bike to Lunch Day" and other bike hikes. Campus Affairs Advisory Board, composed of faculty, administration and elected students, reviewed academic and non-academic affairs of the year. One of their cases involved the illegal publication of the "Freshman Record." Once again Associated Women Students sponsored a Big Sister program for underprivileged children at Christmas. They also planned seminar sessions on topics of interest to women students.

Below Left: **AWS** FRONT ROW: Nancy Glick, Debbie Apato, Alice Quibilan, Pam Greenberg, and Bev Nash. SECOND ROW: Dale Shapiro, Holly Edelman, Roberta Montalto, Debbie Brayton, Andrea Levinson, Madeline Mitchell, Susi Sherman, and Claire Manning. Left: **CAAB** SITTING: Mike York, Linda Chamness, E. J. Ritter, and Carolyn Young. STANDING: Donald M. Albanito, George Armstrong, Max Wessler, and Thomas D. Coker. Below: **Circle K** SITTING: William Riley, Judy Styles, Sue Czerwinski and Lee Matthews. STANDING: Dick DePalma, Stephen Green, and Stephen Tabor.

195

Bradley Chorale is an organization composed of approximately forty individuals who were selected on the basis of auditions. The members of this group received one-half credit per semester for their musical work. In the spring, Chorale traveled to Canada for their annual spring tour.

The Bradley Concert Band used its skill to bring pleasure to university ceremonies and formal events. Students from all parts of the university participated in the Concert Band, as well as in the Jazz Band. This group gave many successful concerts during the year, and added to the excitement of athletic events.

Above: **Chorale** FRONT ROW: Linda Salm, Mary Jane Lilly, Alice Kjar, Rae Jean Perrine, Dr. John Lilly, Jody Bennett, Mary Gower, Denise Adams, Pam Grabel, and Mary Junod. SECOND ROW: Mary Ludwig, Patti Klancer, Sue Edwards, Courtney Campbell, Pam Speer, Diane Rigley, Aldie Jakus, Judy Hucker, and Sheryl Solomon. THIRD ROW: Lynn Puffer, Debbie Harn, Rick Carroll, Greg Smith, Roman Wegrzyn, Don Valente, John Davis, Jim Long, Mary Potts, and Patti Moore. BACK ROW: Rick McElvaine, Jerry Hadley, Jeff Milligan, Ron Krause, Larry Bowie, Kevin Maynor, Forrest Keaton, Steve Curry, Kim Michael, Steve Focken, and Larry McKee. *Above right:* **Concert Band** FRONT ROW: Assistant Director Donald Perrilles, Gene Williams, Tom Hallett, Denise Adams, Phyllis Thomas, Wendy Eisenberg, Lynn Forster, Marlene Francel, Janice Klimala, Judi Ross, and Director Dr. Harold Pottenger. SECOND ROW: Daryl Bear, Mary Walsh, Matt Scheffler, Mike Chapman, Greg Goyen, Jay Lawrence, Tom Bueschel, Shannon Billings, John Gupton, Dick Kandiko, Tom Platt, Sandy Syfert, Kathy Nance, Jean Rogers, Dennis Stewart,

Larry Gibes, Debbie Dimmick, Roy Ginsberg, and Alan Sunshine. THIRD ROW: Kerry Fields, Gerry Malzone, Lynn D'Altorio, Cheryl Peterson, Jeff Crohn, Robert Reilly, Gary Kessler, Mark Magdule, Darrell Stoddard, Wayne Lapen, Rod Sabick, Ken Schoepf, Dean Capretti, Randy Stone, Tim Beranek, Gary Anna, Rich Roth, John Cowie, Jan Kirkel, and Cliff Smith. BACK ROW: Bill Straus, John Mahoney, Keith Killgo, Bill Shelby, Judy Muller, Bill Engstrom, Joe Goble, Meredith Sweet, Rick Carroll, Lee Wilson, David Stieglitz, Rick Coates, Holly Miller, Roger Ruthhart, Bill Silfies, Don Valente, Duane Lindsey, Dave Dunn, Greg Reigel, Tom Banks, Rick Bisping, and Mark Hanson. *Right:* **Jazz Band** FRONT ROW: Don Bawer. SECOND ROW: Rob Reilly, Dave Stieglitz, Keith Killgo, Judy Muller, John Mahoney, Judi Ross, Gene Williams, Sandy Syfert, Richard Kandiko, Kathy Nance, Wayne Lapen, and Jeff Crohn. SECOND ROW: Bill Strauss, Don Perrilles, Mark Hanson, Rick Bisping, Greg Reigel, Tom Banks, Duane Lindsey, and Daryl Bear. THIRD ROW: Jan Kirkel, Cliff Smith, Tim Beranek, and Dean Capretti.

CHEERLEADING *tryouts required girls to perform two cheers before judges.*

Bradley's Cheerleaders added enthusiasm and spirit to basketball games. The excitement and dirve they showed through cheers, rhythmic clapping, flips, jumps, and splits helped the players to perform better and made for an exciting season. The Meri-N-Ettes acted as ushers who seated the crowd before the games, and added color and enjoyment to half-time with their many different dances and drills.

Above **Cheerleaders** FRONT ROW: Cynthia Kilpatrick, Robin Friedlander, and Jacqueline McLean. SECOND ROW: Cyndee Blundell, Valerie McElroy, Donnita Anderson, and Kathy Kimpling. BACK ROW: Charles Wright and Gerald Clark. *Far left* **Meri-N-Ettes** FRONT ROW: Lynn Demanes, Patty McClane, Mary McClane, Ailene Comeaux, Debbie Dahlen, Julie Buck, and Joan Niemeier. SECOND ROW: Maryrose Savage, Patty Quinn, Diane Saelens, Diane Parke, Sue Bruce, and Deb Keeley. BACK ROW: Carolyn Jirka, Alice Karmasin, Marla Duke, Valerie Hughes, Kelly Ford, and Cindy Janota.

ANOTHER two for the Braves and everyone cheers with the seven cheerleaders.

Independent Student Association

1. Bob Giles Ganey
2. Kevin Ford
3. Bob Zyskowski
4. Cindy Royer
5. Charlie Tarjan
6. Debbie Hardy
7. Sherry Sisco
8. Head (Gerry Klimek)
9. Barb Salins
10. Roger Lucero
11. Ed Schavitz
12. Dale Murawski
13. Ace Van Zuiden
14. Chuck Waterbury
15. Tom Koslosky
16. Jimmy Perz
17. P.J.

Publications Council consists of students and faculty members who act as an advisory group to the Anaga and the Scout, in the selection of editors and business staff, and the planning of the budgets. This year the Publications Board prosecuted the Student Center Board for illegal publication of The Freshman Record. Radio Advisory Council consists of students and faculty members who supervise the management, personnel, and development of WCBU, Bradley's campus radio station.

Below: **Publications Board** STANDING: Dr. William Steiner, Mr. Henry Baker, Linda Paul, Daryl Glick, and Dr. Max Wessler. SITTING: Bruce Kopetz. Bottom: **Radio Advisory Council** Frank Thomas, Jim Tanker, Joel Hartman, and Don Markley.

BRADLEY *SCOUT*

In their continuing effort to establish credibility, the Scout tried to overcome past biases. Operating under financial difficulties, the newspaper staff spent about 60 hours of work on each issue. A special issue on the security staff was put out to try to inform students of happenings on campus. And the final words of NO COMMENT rounded out the year of interviewing.

Right: **Scout Reporters and Photographers** FRONT ROW: Rick Waldmeier, Val Green, Dan Ball, Don Vincz, Mike McKune, and Jim Ruppert. ON LADDER: Kathy Maiman, Cathy Weinrich, Phoebe Ferris, Roger Ruthhart, and Craig Brown. *Above right:* **Scout Business Managers:** Ben Kelley, Kevin Bielik, Glen Baldwin, Wayne Schupp, Tom Bicknell, and Tom Sunyan. *Below right:* **Scout Editorial Staff** STANDING: Michael Gebben, Dave Fields, Bob Zyskowski, and Bob Marich. KNEELING: Marcia Lewis, Roxie Marshburn, and Sue Istvanek.

ANAGA

New ideas, a creative concept of yearbook design, and chocolate chip cookies characterized the ANAGA. Recruiting almost an entire new staff after two months of work, the usual problems of photography, and mounting deadlines found editors making the office their home.

With Greek problems and organization woes the ladder began to give more and more space to empty pages that filled up with creative ideas.

However, we know that we have a reason to exist because half of the campus bought yearbooks.

ANAGA Staff: Mike Dore, Monica Avery, Mark Eidinger, Laura Judd, MaryBeth Genis, Miriam Smith, Brenda Fleming, Steve Glaser, Peggy Butler, Greg Goyen, Dee Robbins, Barb Salins, Randy Worcester, Kathy Golob, Phil Ceraulo, and Marie Saul.

WCBU, 88.3 FM, this year presented alternative programming seven days a week to Bradley and the surrounding community during new extended hours. Transmitting from Jobst Hall, the large, enthusiastic staff delivered music, news, and entertainment to its diversified audience. As a student-organized and student-run operation, WCBU worked to train students in the practical applications of radio broadcasting.

Above: **WCBU** FRONT ROW: Rob Klein, Rich Mann, Gerry Morris, Preston King, Jr., Gregory Adams, and Walter Theus, Jr. SECOND ROW: Bobb Jelen, Lydia Santiago, Alan Cohan, Susan Zabloudil, and David Dzurak. THIRD ROW: Wayne Tumminello, Scott L. Winzeler, Dan Fergus, Martin Belcke, Tom Nicholson, Peter Rubenstein, Miles Neff, Steven Cartwright and Ken Tarnoff. *Right:* **WCBU Managers** SITTING: Operations Manager John Stewart and Director of Promotion and Development Mark G. Dolnick. STANDING: Technical Manager Ken Hunold, Chief Engineer Emeritus Bernard, Station Manager Frank Thomas, and Music Director Lenard Pearlman.

206

THE last two minutes pass slowly for announcer Peggy Butler.

RA's and ARA's provided help,
counseling, and advice to dorm residents. After filling out applications,
being interviewed, and acting out
their responses to a given situation,
women and men were carefully selected and placed on floors. RA's
act not as disciplinarians, but rather
as older and experienced persons to
turn to with a problem. All staff
members arrived on campus before
school started to attend informative
sessions, and throughout the year
held staff meetings to learn the facts
on drugs, birth control, and other
contemporary issues.

Above: **Harper-Wychoff RA's & ARA's** FRONT ROW: Steve Rowson, Ansel Braynen, and Chuck Wright. SECOND ROW: Tom Wendle, Rich Kolar, Mickey Moen, Willie Denton, Tommy Elzey, Edward Pryor, Tim Lynch, and Barry Suprenant. BACK ROW: Chip Small, Steve Mueller, Mike Rucker, Steve Young, Frank Freeman, Stan Taraskewich, Jerry Rose, and Mike Babula. *Above left:* **Lovelace-Sisson RA's & ARA's** FRONT *ROW:* Dann Lobsinger, Mike Weiler, Tim Wendie, and Dale Anderson. BACK ROW: Steve Zaleski and Mike Gebben. *Left:* **Heitz RA's & ARA's** FRONT ROW: Peggy Kistler, Susie Andich, and Linda Anderson. SECOND ROW: Sharon Bull, Kerry Murphy, and Sheryl Bull. BACK ROW: Sherrye Zimmerman, Cindy Cooper, and Jeanne McShane.

Arnold Air Society FRONT ROW: Chaplain Tom Hudock, *Executive officer* Michael Pribilski, *Commander* Neil Stuart, *Recorder* Mark Rogers, and *Operations Officer* Forrest Keaton. SECOND ROW: Robert Baer Jr., Robert Wicke, Dan Foreman, Jim Stauner, Glenn Miyahira, Michael Salmi, *Administrative Officer* Bob Marler, and Troy Pombert. THIRD ROW: Mark Cluskey, Robert Mitchell, Nancy Knowles, Robert Klein, Cyndee Possley, John Piepenbrink, Leon Ploszaj, Stanley Eddleman, Jeffrey Graves, Paul Varga, and James Greathouse. BACK ROW: Howard Ferry, Joseph Zeman, Jay Barr, Donald Edwards, Gerald Bockenek, Roger Ouellette, Cal Coolidge, Ted Bushong, Dave Lenzi, and Venn Heerman.

Angel Flight FRONT ROW: Bev Nash, Administrative Officer Sue Woods, Commander Karen Fortuna, Information Officer Debbie Stein, and Nancy Kistler. SECOND ROW: Darla Brown, Dottie D'Angelo, Carol Belbach, Glenda Trollope, Susan Wood, Ann Gysin, Carolyn Young, and Major Llyod Filkins. BACK ROW: Historian Sue Pulte, Standard Officer Joy Schroederus, Cyndee Possley, Operations Officer Jody Bennett, Liaison Officer Nancy Knowles, and Alice Quibilan.

Arnold Air Society is an honorary for men in AFROTC and Angel Flight is a national honorary service sorority that serves as their auxiliary.

A main part of their activities involve the youth of the Peoria area. They entertain children in the hospital at holidays and serve as Big Brothers and Sisters to delinquent children. They offer their skills as resources for Explorer Scouts.

MEMBERS of Arnold Air Society fill out forms at one of their weekly meetings.

213

Vets Club FRONT ROW: *Dennis Saffrin, James Davies, Larry Batten, Dave Long, Bill Shamick, Bob Raz,* and *Mike Scott.* SECOND ROW: *Del Nannen, Kim Ottarson, Dick Taber, Rick Williams, John Church,* and *Dennis Kleinau.*

Vets Club is a social organization designed to make entry into college life easier for the returning veteran. It sponsored various activities such as smokers, slop parties, a spring picnic, and a dinner dance. Members were also able to participate in bowling, basketball, and other intramural sports on campus.

VETS compete with other organizations such as ISA through intramural sports.

SPORTS participation is one part of the Vets' activities.

Alpha Phi Omega

1. Art Moshure
2. John Swidergal
3. Mark Hoffman
4. Scott Kuhlmey
5. Wally Buzlaff
6. Jan Sorrentino
7. John Breitsamater
8. Ira Schuldman
9. Kathy Mott
10. Greg Cwik
11. Ellen Dougherty
12. Carole Crane
13. Charlene Fitzgerald
14. Phil Schipper
15. Debbie Luzietti
16. Mike Kretzer
17. Butch Hopkins
18. Bruce Plassemeyer
19. Bill Welsch
20. Jim Ladd
21. Karen Canter
22. Jim Keeney

23. Sherwin Rankin
24. Phyllis Raphael
25. Barbara Carvell
26. Howard Levin
27. Doug Robertson
28. Ann Frediani
29. Dennis Saffrin
30. Joanne Gilbert
31. Sheryle Block
32. Gary Wilson
33. Tom Johnston
34. Ray Parson
35. Larry Bielicke
36. Bob Mitchell
37. Rich Roth
38. Jon Felshaw
39. Caroline Roberts
40. Jeanne Mayworm
41. Aldie Jakus
42. Tim Pifko
43. Paul Rachielles

Gamma Sigma Phi

1. Lina Zink
2. Linda Anderson
3. Barb Mott
4. Ellen Sohn
5. Jill Finke
6. Ann Dooley
7. Nancy Scherer
8. Linda Mainero
9. Jane Walder
10. Sally Seher
11. Joan McGrath
12. Jeanine Peterson
13. Terri Bielicke
14. Janet Rattberg
15. Peggy Batka
16. Linda Cohn
17. Judy Larson
18. Linda Olander
19. Linda Eastman
20. Sancee Siebold
21. Charlene Fitzgerald
22. Sheila Fogarty
23. Mary McLaughlin
24. Wendy Estrin
25. Bev Nash
26. Amy Kaspar
27. Terri Corrigan
28. Debby Brayton
29. Gail Hopkins
30. Patti Hanlon
31. Maricela Lamcran
32. Diane Jennings
33. Carol Feist
34. Debby Steele
35. Myrna Lindberg
36. Joannie Wilson
37. Lisa Benjamin
38. Nadine Miller
39. Diana Hauter
40. Kathy Kovacic

217

Right: **Hillel** FRONT ROW: Bruce Opdycke, Secretary Roz Gentle, Carol Levinson, Jodie Weintraub, and Martin Kamner. SECOND ROW: Nancy Holtzman, Shelley Gordon, and Treasurer Howard Levin. THIRD ROW: Irving Kahn, Marla Jacobb, Barb Shelton, Peter Hesky, Phyllis Raphael, and Jay Lawrence. FOURTH ROW: Roy Ginsberg, Kenneth Tarnoff, Glenn Smoler, Vice President Larry Rose, and Advisor Dr. Katz. *Below:* **Newman Club** FRONT ROW: Barb Miller, Eugene Wojtas, and Sue Kaldahl. SECOND ROW: Rick Smith, Jo Anne Hostatter, Fran Spinillo, Deb Fowler, Ray Figlewicz, John Finneran, and Stan Radosevich. THIRD ROW: Barb Rodgers, Mike Grzywa, Wayne Lampen, Don Hovik, Al Jaskunas, and Tom Lebak. *Far right:* **Intervarsity Christian Fellowship** FRONT ROW: Nancy Hambee, Vice President Becky Fairly, Secretary Kris Brown, and Laurel Taylor. SECOND ROW: Jan Crego, Kim Allison, Jody Iftner, Mascot Jane Bennett, and Peggy Kistler. THIRD ROW: Bernie Potempa, Treasurer Mike Pawlik, Nancy Hamby, Publicity Chairman Betsy Beckwith, Judy Malan, President Greg McCoy, and Emma Wittig. FOURTH ROW: Dale Nobel, Pete Odon, Missions Chairman Dane Dunn, Lolly Bunton, Rick Schmutz, Book Chairman Ken Spaulding, Bill Corra, Mark Malan (Staff), and Steve Spencer. FIFTH ROW: Mark Thomas, Advisor Dr. Thomas Cummings, Mark Larson, John Wolber, and Dennis Hill.

218

B'nai B'rith Hillel provided for the needs and concerns of the Jewish student on Bradley's campus. It kept the student close to his faith by providing religious services and discussions. Newman Club offered a place for Catholic students to live, study, and talk. Through the Masses they held on campus every Sunday morning, Newman Club helped draw Bradley students and the Catholic community together. Inter-Varsity Christian Fellowship served to help the modern Christian learn more about his religion through various activities such as Bible studies and weekly meetings.

Alpha Lambda Delta, national honorary for freshman women, took its members from girls with a 7.0 overall gradepoint. Chimes, the junior women's honorary, admitted second semester sophomores and all junior women with a 5.5 overall gradepoint and have shown leadership and service qualities. Mortar Board, national honorary for senior women, based its membership on a 6. overall gradepoint and leadership in extra-curricular activities. This year the group took charge of planning the annual ODK leadership conference.

Left: **Alpha Lambda Delta** SITTING: Valerie Hughes, Nancy Kistler, and Lynda Willer. STANDING: Mary Jane Lilly, Cathy Weinrich, Donna Malmgren, and Debra Leeper. Below left: **Mortar Board** SEATED: Barb Bergman. STANDING: Roslyn Murphy, Carolyn Young, Terese Naddy, Barb Bredel, Helen Czachorski, Dorothy Coover, Jan Moranz, and Joan Koch. Below: **Chimes** SITTING: Lillian Glass, Lynda Willer, Nancy Scherer, Colette Gronczewski, Elizabeth Jagoda, Mardona Thornton, and Darilyn Caskey. STANDING: Nancy Knowles, Amyre Coleman, Madeline Mitchell, Joan Myers, Mari Jo Smith, Corky Pfiester, Lee Ann Kozak, Carol Kearny, and Laura Judd.

Who's Who is a group of students chosen for their outstanding scholastic records and leadership in extra-curricular activities. One percent of the nation's college students are eligible for consideration. Twenty-three students from Bradley were chosen. ·

Above left: Linda Chamness, Al Lipperini, Lillian Glas, Rick Andrulis, Darilyn Caskey, Patrick Baikauskas, Thomas Pisano posing for Tim Engen, Jeff Hughes, Jeanne McShane, Doe Coover, Gordon Tingley, and Barbara Musielak. *Below left:* Tim Engen. *Below:* Tom Lebak, Carol Kearney, Edward Meyer, Helen Czachorski, Judy Larson, Joan Myers, Jacie Levy, and Gerald Pfeiffer.

Construction Club SEATED: Mike Golden and Frank Inzinna. FIRST ROW: Tom Bleigh, Ron Lockwood, Bob Laskl, and Edward Schavitz. SECOND ROW: Clark Sauer, Larry Biellcke, David Olszak, and John Ohl. THIRD ROW: Patrick Callahan, John Breltsameter, John Harchut, Bill Shelby, and John Egan. BACK ROW: James Adrian, Allred Parthum, M. I. Guest, F. E. Rebholz, and Steven Brown.

Construction Club made it possible for students in engineering and technology to become acquainted with the practical aspects of their studies. Throughout the year, members heard guest speakers from Caterpillar and other industries, saw films on highway systems, and took trips to plants and construction sights. Construction Club also organized a library of magazines and other references to help students through their engineering courses.

Construction Club SEATED: Mike Golden and
Frank Inzinna. FIRST ROW: Tom Bleigh, Ron
Lockwood, Bob Laski, and Edward Schavitz.
SECOND ROW: Clark Sauer, Larry Bielicke,
David Olszak, and John Ohl. THIRD ROW:
Patrick Callahan, John Breltsameter, John
Harchut, Bill Shelby, and John Egan. BACK
ROW: James Adrian, Alfred Parthum, M
Guest, F. E. Rebholz, and Steven Brown

COMMENTARY

It was a year of apathy — nothing happened. No one cared about the war, no one cared about pollution, no one cared about a candidate for anything, no one cared about POWs, no one cared about women's liberation, no one cared about the economic situation. In short nothing happened because no one made it happen.

Everyone seemed to be playing the game of who could be seen on campus the least number of times.

Party time lasted from the Friday night get-together through the Saturday night orgy. Then there was Wednesday (celebrate the middle of the week), Thursday (celebrate the coming weekend), Sunday (prolong the weekend), which left Monday and Tuesday as appropriate days to celebrate anything.

There was always drugs, booze or sex to help forget the hassle with a roommate or that F in philosophy.

But what did you really do while you were here for four years? Was it worth it?

Well, let's see, there was always Si's or Mecca — places to meet old friends and new ones. You probably attended at least one basketball game in four years. Your boyfriend/girlfriend can now stay in your room 24 hours. You changed from that blue marker of freshman year to a yellow one.

How many times was it you tried to cash a check without your I.D. card? How many paperbacks do you have stacked up that the bookstore won't take back or how many textbooks that professors decided not to use the next year that the bookstore wouldn't buy back?

You saw the rise and fall of one of the best things ever at Bradley — a student owned-student run business — B.S.S., Inc., which departed due to lack of student interest and support. You saw the end of football and homecoming. Tuition went up and up. Van Arsdale went from president to chancelor. The 75th anniversary of the university came and went with no fanfare.

You watched the activism of the 60's evolve into the apathy of the 70's.

And now you're finally going to graduate and find success and happiness in life because you own a college degree. At least that's the myth they all told you when you thought about going to college and when you entered.

How can it really be that so much (so little) happened in so short a time??

Chancellor Van Arsdale

Dr. Talman W. Van Arsdale, Jr. has been Bradley's first Chancellor since June, 1971. He represents Bradley in negotiations with patrons who provide financial assistance to the university. Dr. Van Arsdale previously served as Bradley's sixth president from 1961 until 1970.

President Martin C. Abegg

CAPS and gowns are the graduation
day attire for administrators, too.

FILLING the president's chair for his second year,
President Abegg conducts business in his office.

"YOU'RE the president?!"

226

BRADLEY UNIVERSITY

PEORIA, ILLINOIS 61606

ing the past year, Bradley University celebrated the
sary of its founding by Mrs. Lydia Moss Bradley in 1897.
theme for the year's celebration, "Building on a Proud
choes well of the past and sets the tone for the future.

st certainly, over the past 75 years, the University has
roud heritage and stands today as an educational institu-
ity and distinction. It has reached this position as a
cial support, and hard work of many
or another, not only contributed, but also
iversity's existence and development.

I prepare this letter for the 1973 Anaga, I am tempted
e over my 25 years as a part of Bradley University but as
so succinctly stated, "The Past is Prologue", and so as I
future, I am sure that the University will continue to
roud heritage and that 25 years hence when the University
its 100th Anniversary, we can again look   with pride
ction on the efforts accomplished.

Martin G. Abegg
President

President's

Vice President
Richard M. Trumpe

Vice President
George B. Ferguson

Academic Affairs Vice President George Ferguson is involved in all university instructional matters such as scheduling of classes and use of instructional facilities.

He is head of all the Deans and Directors of the ten various schools and colleges in the university and leads the directors of: Black Studies, Institutional Research and Registrar, the Library, the Scholars' Program, and the Center for Learning Resources.

Dr. Ferguson is Chairman of the Committee on Honorary Degrees and in addition, serves in the capacity of university president when Dr. Abegg is away from campus.

Vice President
George R. Beck

In charge of University Business Affairs, George Beck is chief fiscal officer and corporate Secretary-Treasurer of Bradley.

He coordinates all matters pertaining to university business and of committees regarding endowment.

Among the personnel under Mr. Beck are: Assistant Treasurer and Controller, Director of Purchasing, Superintendent of Buildings and Grounds, and Bookstore Manager.

As head of Student Services Office, Vice President Trumpe organizes the efforts of all full-time professional staff employed to assist each student and group on all matters affecting student well-being.

Dr. Trumpe is responsible for coordinating the following departments: Dean of Men's Office, Dean of Women's Office, Counseling Center, Student Center and Student Activities, Student Financial Aid, Placement, Housing, Health Center and Security Office for the campus.

Committee

Dean of Admissions
Orville Nothdurft

Controller
Joseph F. Mele

The office of Assistant Treasurer and Controller provides numerous financial services for the student body. Mr. Mele's staff maintains student and campus organizations accounts, cashes checks, issues student insurance, handles all veterans' accounts, and grants student loans under certain circumstances.

Other duties, including the handling of all tuition, the issuing of all payroll checks and the maintenance of the Personnel Office are also in Mr. Mele's charge.

Executive Secretary
A. G. "Frenchie"
Haussler

As the University's Executive Secretary, Dr. Haussler works most extensively on the Deferred Giving Program in which he advises patrons who wish to bequeath financial aid to Bradley in their last wills.

"Frenchie" Haussler is also Secretary of the Activities Committee of the Board of Trustees.

Recruiting new students for Bradley from high schools and junior colleges across the country is the most time-consuming duty of Dean of Admissions Orville Nothdurft.

Through Mr. Nothdurft's office counseling of all prospective high school and transfer students is conducted along with the gathering and judging of data and credentials of applicants.

A large part of the Admissions Director's job also deals with public relations. Therefore, Dean Nothdurft delivers a large number of speeches and serves on several panels throughout the year representing and endorsing Bradley University.

Vice President's Committee for Student Services

BACK ROW: Vice President for Student Services Richard Trumpe, Director of Placement Robert Pardieck, Director of Orientation Ray Zarvell, Director of Financial Aid Thomas Cromwell, Dean of Men Edward King, Director of Student Center E. J. Ritter, Jr., Director of Security Office Curley Johnson, Director of Counseling Center Dr. Harold R. Miller, and Director of Housing Kenneth Goldin. SEATED IN FRONT: Dean of Women Camille Primm.

Vice President's Committee for Academic Affairs

SITTING: Assoc. Professor of Education Virgil Grunkemeyer, Director of the School of 'Speech and Hearing Sciences James Mullendore, Professor of Mechanical Engineering Harold Ratcliff, Student Representative Barb Bergman, Acting Dean of the College of Business Administration Richard Hartman, and Dean of the College of Engineering and Technology Peter Bulkeley. STANDING: Vice President for Academic Affairs George Ferguson, Dean of the College of Education Leo Bent, Dean of the Graduate School Wilbur Grimm, Assoc. Professor of Biology Gerald Elseth, Student Representative Dick Bardoulas, Director of the School of Music Allen Cannon, Instructor in Foreign Languages Penny Pucelik, Professor of History Lester Brune, Assoc. Professor of Business Administration Paul Arney, and Dean of the College of Continuing Education Donald Albanito.

'72 Putnam Award Winner
Dr. Richard Bjorklund, Biology

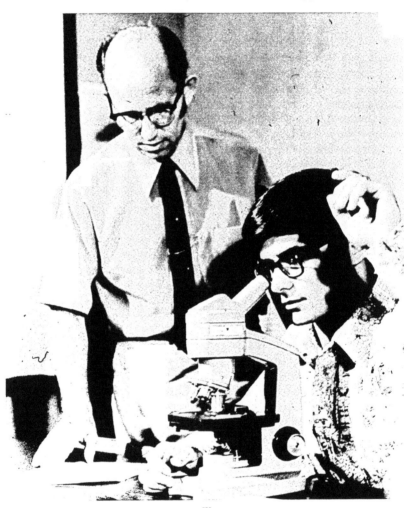

Seniors

Gregory Adams
Electronics Technology
Chicago, Ill.

Anthony Agatucci
Biology
East Peoria, Ill.

Jeffrey Alexander
Political Science
Washington, Ill.

Phyllis Alexander
Economics
Chicago, Ill.

Daniel Allen
Law
Rockford, Ill.

Rodney Allen
Business Man. & Admin.
Ashland, Ill.

Caryn Alverdy
Sociology
Chicago, Ill.

Dale Anderson
English
Wheaton, Ill.

Linda Anderson
Art
Oak Lawn, Ill.

Russell Anderson
Electronics Technology
Oak Lawn, Ill.

Susan Andich
Special Education
Rock Island, Ill.

Francine Aranow
Sociology
Hollywood, Fla.

Ryan Armbruster
Economics & Pol. Science
Tinley Park, Ill.

James Ascot
Speech
Chicago, Ill.

Bonnie Atwood
Home Economics
Grand Ridge, Ill.

Andrew Bachler
Electronics Technology
Zion, Ill.

John Baird
Mechanical Engineering
Peoria, Ill.

Gary Baker
Electronics Technology
Monroe Center, Ill.

Norma Balentine
Journalism
Peoria, Ill

Louise Barber
Education
Metamora, Ill.

Irwin Barg
Business Man. & Admin.
Houston, Tex.

Christopher Barnes
Political Science
Washington, D.C

Richard Barnett
Political Science
Clifton, N.J

Jay Barr
Construction Technology
Chesterfield, Ill.

233

Pamela Barr
Elementary Education
Peoria, Ill.

Charles Barron
Business Man. & Admin.
Chicago, Ill.

Michael Bashkin
International Studies
Chicago, Ill.

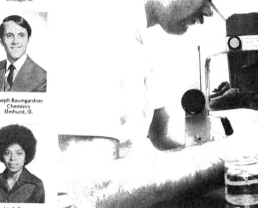

Larry Batten
Electronics Technology
Silvis, Ill.

Joseph Baumann
Civil Engineering
Peoria, Ill.

Joseph Baumgardner
Chemistry
Elmhurst, Ill.

Marvin Bausman
Physics
Mt. Carroll, Ill.

Zachary Bay
Political Science
Skokie, Ill.

Linda Bean
Physical Education
Washington, D.C.

Daryl Bear
Music Education
Cinnaminson, N.J.

Jack Becker
Sociology
E. Peoria, Ill.

Elizabeth Beckwith
English
Peoria, Ill.

Robert Behlke
Electrical Technology
Rolling Meadows, Ill.

Rex Bell
Retailing & Marketing
Wilmington, Ill.

Steven Bennett
Engine Power Technology
Rockford, Ill.

Teresa Benson
Biology
Peoria, Ill.

Robert Bergamasco
Sociology
White Plains, N.Y.

Robert Berger
Political Science
Brooklyn, N.Y.

Barbara Bergman
History & Pol. Science
Peoria, Ill.

Kathleen Beske
English
Chicago, Ill.

Jerome Bielicke
Journalism
E. St. Louis, Ill.

234

Lawrence Bielicke
Construction Technology
E. St. Louis, Ill.

Barry Bilder
English
Peoria, Ill.

Nihat Bilgutay
Electronics Technology
Peoria, Ill.

Richard Bisping
Electronics Technology
Peotone, Ill.

Robert Blackledge
Mechanical Engineering
Hamilton, Ill.

Donald Blackman
Engine Power Technology
Chicago, Ill.

Thomas Bleigh
Construction Technology
Hannibal, Mo.

Karenne Bloomgarden
Physical Education
Livingston, N.J.

Gerald Bockenek
Psychology
Westwood, N.J.

Frances Bocox
English
Chicago, Ill.

Peter Boehme
Sociology
Port Washington, N.Y.

Alice Bolt
Special Education
Hanna City, Ill.

Stuart Borden
English
Wyoming, Ill.

John Bortko
Retailing & Marketing
Hillside, Ill.

Gary Bouchard
Civil Engineering
Herscher, Ill.

Robert Boyd
Sociology
Lacon, Ill.

Robert Boyer
Civil Engineering
Quincy, Ill.

Jeffrey Brady
Mechanical Engineering
Arlington Heights, Ill.

Richard Brandeis
Retailing & Marketing
Riverside, Ill.

Clay Bray
Biology
Chicago, Ill.

Katherine Bredel
Business Man. & Admin.
Peoria, Ill.

John Bredemeyer
Electronics Technology
Peoria, Ill.

Mark Breitman
Sociology
West Orange, N.J.

Gene Brieske
Retailing & Marketing
Chicago, Ill.

Gary Brooks
Psychology
Washington, D.C.

Bruce Brown
Business Man. & Admin.
Skokie, Ill.

Steven Brown
Construction Technology
Peoria, Ill.

Charles Brunner
Mathematics
Tremont, Ill.

Harry Bryan
Electronics Technology
Normal, Ill.

Richard Buchanan
Political Science
Des Plaines, Ill.

235

Paul Buck
Mechanical Engineering
Kankakee, Ill.

James Buckert
Biology
Warsaw, Ill.

Sharon Bullis
Home Economics
Earlville, Ill.

Walter Burzlaff
Retailing & Marketing
Aurora, Ill.

Barbara Butterfield
Art
Peoria, Ill.

Barbara Candice
International Studies
Chicago, Ill.

Bruce Carmaney
Electronics Technology
Geneseo, Ill.

Robert Carroll
Art
Park Ridge, Ill.

Darilynn Caskey
Political Science
Bartonville, Ill.

John Catlin
Electronics Technology
Peoria, Ill.

Orlando Ceaser
Biology
Chicago, Ill.

Martin Ceranec
History
Berwyn, Ill.

John Cerkvenik
Engine Power Technology
Hometown, Ill.

Judith Chambers
Sociology
Henry, Ill.

Linda Chamness
History
Belleville, Ill.

Donald Chaplin
Chemistry
Peoria, Ill.

Edith Chittum
English
Findlay, Ill.

Nhoth Chouravong
Mechanical Engineering
Jacksonville, Ill.

Donna Chrisman
Home Economics
Peoria, Ill.

Loren Christophel
Engine Power Technology
Delavan, Ill.

James Clark
Electronics Technology
Silvis, Ill.

Mark Clark
Retailing & Marketing
Rockford, Ill.

Stephen Clark
Art
Morton, Ill.

Douglas Clausen
Electronics Technology
Rock Island, Ill.

Diane Cohen
English
Skokie, Ill.

Larry Cohen
Economics
Nashville, Tenn.

Richard Cohen
Business Man. & Admin.
Milwaukee, Wis.

Helene Cohn
Speech & Hearing
Highland Park, N.J.

Linda Cohn
Art
Chicago, Ill.

Jack Collins
Accounting
Berkeley, Mo.

Joseph Conklin
Physical Education
Lakewood, N.J.

James Connolly
Retailing & Marketing
Somonauk, Ill.

Lynn Conover
History
Port Washington, N.Y.

Evajean Conroy
Art
Arlington Heights, Ill.

Martin Conway
Business Man. & Admin.
McHenry, Ill.

Timothy Conway
Biology
Woodstock, Ill.

Franci Cook
Physical Education
Skokie, Ill.

Kristine Coologeorgen
Elementary Education
Peoria Heights, Ill.

Earnest Cooper
Art
Chicago, Ill.

Dorothy Coover
English
Chicago, Ill.

Augustus Corley
English
Falls Church, Va.

Richard Cornwall
Engine Power Technology
Downers Grove, Ill.

Robert Corrigan
Construction Technology
Hinsdale, Ill.

Marsha Coulson
Speech & Hearing
Peoria, Ill.

Paul Creamer
Sociology
Peoria Heights, Ill.

Charlene Crusoe
Sociology
Peoria, Ill.

Paul Curran
Accounting
Palos Heights, Ill.

Joe Curtis
Business Man. & Admin.
Honolulu, Hi.

John Czaplewski
Engine Power Technology
Chicago, Ill.

Richard Dallinger
Chemistry
Morton, Ill.

James DalSanto
Business Man. & Admin.
Rockford, Ill.

Edward Dassow
Political Science
Chicago, Ill.

David Davies
Industrial Engineering
Naperville, Ill.

James Davies
Construction Technology
Peoria, Ill.

Diane Davis
Elementary Education
Chesterfield, Mo.

Kathryn Davis
Art
Chicago, Ill.

Larry Davis
Electrical Engineering
Huntley, Ill.

Larry Decker
Industrial Engineering
Lincoln, Ill.

Lynnette Demanes
Psychology
Peoria, Ill.

Beverly Disabato
French
Blue Island, Ill.

Thomas Dodd
Psychology
Indianapolis, Ind.

Charles Dolan
Spanish
Park Ridge, Ill.

Ellen Dougherty
Speech Pathology
Hazleton, Pa.

Barbara Drake
Sociology
Fort Worth, Tex.

Charla Draper
Home Economics
Chicago, Ill.

Jill Dulman
Sociology
Melrose Park, Ill.

Darlene Dunn
Speech Pathology
Kingston Mines, Ill.

JoAnne Dunne
Elementary Education
Peoria, Ill.

Jeffrey Dunst
Sociology
Peoria, Ill.

Patricia Dwyer
Elementary Education
Peoria, Ill.

Michael Eagan
Industrial Engineering
Newburgh, Ill.

Linda Eastman
Speech & Hearing
Carrollton, Tex.

Annette Eckert
History & Pol. Science
Peoria, Ill.

Morris Eddy
Journalism
Winnetka, Ill.

Carla Edwards
Biology
Chicago, Ill.

Donald Edwards
Economics
Zion, Ill.

John Egan
Construction Technology
Palos Park, Ill.

Fred Einbinder
History
Skokie, Ill.

Howard Elies
Accounting
Northbrook, Ill.

Robert Eligman
Physics
Reading, Pa.

Kenneth Elster
Special Education
Chicago, Ill.

238

Ted Epand
Psychology
Spring Valley, N.Y.

Terri Erlinger
Home Economics
Carlyle, Ill.

Larry Ethun
Electronics Technology
Rockton, Ill.

Michael Evans
Business Man. & Admin.
Chicago, Ill.

Steven Everhart
Electronics Technology
Middlefield, Conn.

Michele Ewing
Speech & Hearing
Silver Spring, Md

Richard Failla
Construction Technology
Fairfield, Conn.

Denise Farina
English
Rockford, Ill.

Harry Feldmann
Business Man. & Admin.
Lake Villa, Ill.

Daniel Fergus
International Studies
St. Louis, Mo.

Joseph Ferry
Engine Power Technology
Port Murray, N.J.

Raymond Figlewicz
Accounting
Chicago, Ill.

Ronda Fine
Elementary Education
Winnetka, Ill.

Jill Finke
Elementary Education
Evanston, Ill.

Karen Fisher
History
Clayton, Mo.

Robert Fisher
Retailing & Marketing
Williamsville, N.Y.

Mary Fleming
Psychology
Chicago, Ill.

Melvin Floyd
Engine Power Technology
Chicago, Ill.

Karen Fortuna
Economics
Chicago, Ill.

Randey Foss
Physical Education
Chicago, Ill.

Peter Francini
Retailing & Marketing
Stratford, Conn.

Barbara Frank
Elementary Education
Highland Park, Ill.

Steven Fransene
Retailing & Marketing
Woodhull, Ill.

Wendi Freedman
Speech & Hearing
Arlington Heights, Ill.

Alan Friedman
Business Man. & Admin.
Denver, Colo.

Gloria Friedman
Home Economics
University City, Mo.

Diana Fritz
English
Peoria, Ill.

Charles Frizzell
Electronics Technology
Granite City, Ill.

Michael Frye
Construction Technology
Aledo, Ill.

Lynn Gaertner
English
Blue Island, Ill.

Marcia Gage
Sociology
Chicago, Ill.

Linda Gaida
English
Peoria, Ill.

Robert Ganey
Construction Technology
Glenview, Ill.

Jacqueline Gardner
Accounting
Chicago, Ill.

William Gaston
Chemistry
Edwardsville, Ill.

Judith Gau
Elementary Education
Milwaukee, Wis.

Joyce Gauthier
English
Waukegan, Ill.

David Gehrt
Electronics Technology
Speer, Ill.

Geri Gellerman
Physical Education
Rock Island, Ill.

Frank Gentile
Business Man. & Admin.
Flossmoor, Ill.

Candice Gerber
Elementary Education
Memphis, Tenn.

Jennifer Gibbar
Art
Peoria, Ill.

Kenneth Gihring
Electrical Engineering
Moro, Ill.

William Gilbert
Mechanical Engineering
Lincoln, Ill.

John Ginder
Industrial Distribution
Metamora, Ill.

Eileen Ginsburg
Retailing & Marketing
Pubbock, Tex.

Michele Glickman
French
Creve Coeur, Mo.

Mary Glidden
English
Kewanee, Ill.

Joseph Goble
Music Education
Westfield, Ill.

Kristine Goebel
Home Economics
Des Plaines, Ill.

Michael Golden
Construction Technology
West Chicago, Ill.

Barry Goldfine
Psychology
Chicago, Ill.

David Goldstein
Political Science
Cleveland Heights, O.

Linda Gomes
English
Eden, Ill.

Bruce Goodman
Political Science
St. Paul, Minn.

William Goodwin
Engine Power Technology
Peoria, Ill.

Judith Gora
Elementary Education
Calumet City, Ill.

Roger Gordon
Economics
Washington, D.C.

Paula Gottlieb
Special Education
Chicago, Ill.

Jerome Gotway
Mechanical Engineering
Hardin, Ill.

240

William Gould
Business Man. & Admin.
Galesburg, Ill.

Ruby Grady
Business Man. & Admin.
Peoria, Ill.

John Gray
Business Man. & Admin.
Barrington, Ill.

Larry Griminger
Political Science
Peoria, Ill.

Leon Grotkowski
Business Man. & Admin.
Chicago, Ill.

John Groy
Electronics Technology
Princeton, Ill.

Howard Gum
Geography & Pol. Science
Sycamore, Ill.

Mary Gunkel
Journalism
Peoria, Ill.

Richard Gunnar
Business Man. & Admin.
Peoria, Ill.

Jon Gurkoff
International Studies
Harrisburg, Pa.

Mark Gurnicz
Philosophy
Schiller Park, Ill.

Martin Hadank
Electrical Engineering
Peoria, Ill.

Alan Haggard
Electrical Engineering
Peoria, Ill.

Carla Haithcox
Mathematics
Chicago, Ill.

Janice Hall
Art
Lima, O.

Melwyn Hallam
Business Man. & Admin.
Peoria, Ill.

Mary Hamilton
Elementary Education
Glenview, Ill.

Richard Handwerg
Electronics Technology
River Vale, N.J.

Hans Hansen
Engine-Power Technology
Chicago, Ill.

William Hansen
Engine Power Technology
Peoria, Ill.

Susan Hardine
Elementary Education
Galesburg, Ill.

241

David Hardy
Construction Technology
Syracuse, N.Y.

Daniel Harmon
Biology
Wheaton, Ill.

David Harrell
Machine Design Tech.
Lombard, Ill.

Andrea Harris
Political Science
Chicago, Ill.

William Hayes
Political Science
Deerfield, Ill.

Margaret Heckinger
Home Economics
Rockford, Ill.

Barbara Heiser
Elementary Education
Peoria, Ill.

Steven Henningson
Geography
St. Charles, Ill

Dorothy Herget
Elementary Education
Peoria, Ill.

Patricia Herschman
International Studies
Hazel Crest, Ill.

John Higgins
Business Man. & Admin.
Dumont, N.J.

David Hill
Engine Power Technology
Stockton, Ill.

Gerald Hinderhan
Business Man. & Admin.
Alton, Ill.

Ray Hodges
Political Science
Chicago, Ill.

Donald Hogeboom
Physical Education
Annawan, Ill.

Gwen Hollowick
Elementary Education
Chicago, Ill.

Ronald Hopkins
Electrical Engineering
Springfield, Ill.

Gregory Hoover
Mechanical Technology
Morton Grove, Ill.

Roberta Hostetler
Speech
Maywood, Ill.

Robert Howard
Civil Engineering
St. Petersburg, Fla.

Jena Howell
Sociology
Washington, Ill.

Carolyn Hull
English
Chicago, Ill.

Carol Humphries
Computer Science & Math.
Springfield, Ill.

Neil Hunter
Sociology
Union, N.J.

Gregory Huss
Biology
Chillicothe, Ill.

Wayne Hyatt
Business Man. & Admin.
Peoria, Ill.

Cynthia Hynes
Speech & Hearing
Calumet City, Ill.

Jo Ellen Iftner
Chemistry
Pittsfield, Ill.

Mark Imber
Psychology
Westbury, N.Y.

George Inglis
Civil Engineering
Highland Park, Ill.

Brent Inman
Accounting
Carlinville, Ill.

Frank Inzinna
Construction Technology
E. Amherst, N.Y.

Louise Irwin
Art
E. Peoria, Ill.

William Irwin
Psychology
Indianapolis, Ind.

Susan Istvanek
Journalism
Chicago, Ill.

David Itken
Engine Power Technology
Sterling, Ill.

Gerald Jackson
Sociology
Chicago, Ill.

Dorian Jefferson
Industrial Engineering
Chicago, Ill.

Linda Jenkins
Mathematics
Springfield, Ill.

Katherine Jetter
Elementary Education
Riverside, Ill.

Carolyn Jirka
German & Mathematics
Downers Grove, Ill.

Jean Jirucha
Home Economics
Georgetown, Conn.

Janet Johns
Accounting
Crystal Lake, Ill.

Carolyn Johnson
Art
E. Moline, Ill.

David Johnson
English
Glencoe, Ill.

Steven Johnson
Engine Power Technology
Silvis, Ill.

Todd Johnson
Industrial Engineering
Rockford, Ill.

Catherine Joiner
Special Education
Tiskilwa, Ill.

Dauris Jones
Elementary Education
Peoria, Ill.

Robert Jones
Industrial Distribution
Springfield, Ill.

Diane Jordt
Physical Education
Elmwood Park, Ill.

Paul Joschko
Business Man. & Admin.
Midlothian, Ill.

Andrew Jost
Accounting
Chicago, Ill.

Gordon Joyner
Economics
Peoria, Ill.

Robert Kamerlander
Accounting
McHenry, Ill.

Arthur Karl
Political Science
Hornell, N.Y.

Richard Katz
Political Science
Chicago, Ill.

Neal Kaufman
Business Man. & Admin.
Chicago, Ill.

Monica Keane
Spanish
Des Plaines, Ill.

Michael Kelly
English
Belvidere, Ill.

Donna Kessinger
Elementary Education
Bartonville, Ill.

Peggy Kistler
Spanish
West Chicago, Ill.

Willie Mae Kitt
Elementary Education
Chicago, Ill.

George Klasek
Psychology
LaGrange Park, Ill.

Dennis Kleinau
Engine Power Technology
Geneseo, Ill.

Gerald Klimek
Electronics Technology
Joliet, Ill.

Stephen Klitzky
Retailing & Marketing
Skokie, Ill.

David Koch
Civil Engineering
Peoria, Ill.

Joan Koch
Elementary Education
Monmouth, Ill.

Carole Konsler
Art
Highland Park, Ill.

Susan Kopel
Business Man. & Admin.
Sioux Falls, S. Dak.

Bruce Kopetz
English
Decatur, Ill.

Benjamin Kopriva
Retailing & Marketing
Mt. Prospect, Ill.

Thomas Koslosky
Business Man. & Admin.
Arlington Heights, Ill.

Marlene Kott
English
Franklin Park, Ill.

Kathleen Kovacic
Home Economics
Lockport, Ill.

John Kovacik
Electrical Engineering
Joliet, Ill.

John Kovarek
Psychology
Chicago, Ill.

244

Jacqueline Kozak
Elementary Education
Chicago, Ill.

Emily Krakow
Retailing & Marketing
Dixon, Ill.

James Kreiser
Psychology
Peoria, Ill.

Richard Kuestner
German
Huntley, Ill.

Scott Kuhlmey
History
Deerfield, Ill.

Ronald Kukral
Construction Technology
Thornton, Ill.

Margaret Kuntz
Elementary Education
Brimfield, Ill.

Linda Kuntzi
Journalism
Springfield, Ill.

Robert Kutik
Retailing & Marketing
Tenafly, N.J.

Thomas Kuzma
Engine Power Technology
Glenview, Ill.

Jonathon Lambert
Electronics Technology
Quincy, Ill.

Wayne Lambert
Construction Technology
Bradley, Ill.

Maria Lane
Special Education
Peoria, Ill.

Thomas Lane
Electrical Engineering
Rockford, Ili.

Judy Larson
Sociology
Clayton, Mo.

Mark Larson
Electrical Engineering
Leland, Ill.

Timothy Laws
Business Man. & Admin.
Kankakee, Ill.

Joseph Layne
Engine Power Technology
Peoria, Ill.

Thomas Lebak
Political Science
Lemont, Ill.

Susan Leeker
Retailing & Marketing
Evanston, Ill.

Lew Leibowitz
Electrical Engineering
Chicago, Ill.

Mark LeMenager
Mathematics
Kankakee, Ill.

Raymond Lemery
Electrical Engineering
Rockford, Ill.

William Leppert
Psychology
S. Elgin, Ill.

Albert Lesko
Biology
Wallington, N.J.

Jaclyn Levy
Elementary Education
St. Louis, Mo.

Wayne Levy
Political Science
Skokie, Ill.

Wendy Levy
Elementary Education
Skokie, Ill.

Rosemarie Lewin
Elementary Education
Hammond, Ind.

Marcia Lewis
Journalism
St. Louis, Mo.

245

Gayle Lieberman
Speech & Hearing
Chicago, Ill.

Bruce Lieblich
Business Man. & Admin.
Hillsdale, N.J.

Lesley Linn
Special Education
Skokie, Ill.

Alfred Lipperini
Law
Kankakee, Ill.

Bruce Little
Sociology
Chicago, Ill.

Randal Livingston
Electrical Engineering
Peoria, Ill.

Dann Lobsinger
Psychology
Dolton, Ill.

Janet Loebs
Business Man. & Admin.
Peoria, Ill.

Roberta Long
Economics
Sudbury, Mass.

Ray Louder
Business Man. & Admin.
Peoria, Ill.

Cheri Loveless
Speech & Hearing
Peoria, Ill.

Robert Lucas
Theatre & Psychology
Peotone, Ill.

Roger Lucero
Chemistry
Batavia, Ill.

Mary Ludwig
Music Education
Lockport, Ill.

Thomas Lumley
Electronics Technology
Reading, Pa.

Donald Lund
Biology
Waukegan, Ill.

Joanne Lynch
Elementary Education
Riverdale, Ill.

William Lyons
Construction Technology
Calumet City, Ill.

Kenneth Maltas
Industrial Engineering
Mount Vernon, O.

Charles Mangene
Electronics Technology
West Sand Lake, N.Y.

Merry Manuel
English
Peoria, Ill.

Hugh Marchmont-Robinson
Chemistry
Evergreen Park, Ill.

Yvonne Marquart
Elementary Education
Bridgeton, Mo.

Marilie Martin
Music Education
Chillicothe, Ill.

Linda Masek
Elementary Education
Peoria, Ill.

Carla Matson
Biology
Kewanee, Ill.

Cynthia Maxon
Art
Libertyville, Ill.

Steven Maze
Electronics Technology
Bellwood, Ill.

Susan McBride
Elementary Education
Rockford, Ill.

Sharon McClenny
Elementary Education
Indianapolis, Ind.

Judith McCoy
Retailing & Marketing
Bethesda, Md.

Michael McCrary
Electronics Technology
Peoria, Ill.

Kathy McDaniels
Art
Pekin, Ill.

David McDermott
Engine Power Technology
Peoria, Ill.

Michael McDonald
Mathematics
Morrison, Ill.

Startreere McDonald
History
Peoria, Ill.

Eleanor McGrath
Biology
Peoria, Ill.

Richard McMicken
Accounting
Elmhurst, Ill.

Jeanne McShane
Special Education
Chicago, Ill.

Daniel Meeker
Industrial Engineering
Peoria, Ill.

Maribeth Meier
Journalism
Park Ridge, Ill

Louis Melendes
Industrial Engineering
Kewanee, Ill.

Richard Mellor
Mechanical Engineering
Peoria, Ill.

Halford Melville
Electrical Engineering
Pekin, Ill.

Daniel Merriman
Business Man. & Admin.
Paw Paw, Ill.

Pamela Meyer
Art
Yonkers, N.Y.

Wendy Meyers
Psychology
Chicago, Ill.

Ronald Mechelsen
Electrical Engineering
Berwyn, Ill.

Harvard Middleton
Journalism
Chicago, Ill.

Judith Miller
Chemistry
Morton, Ill.

247

Margaret Miller
Mathematics
Springfield, Ill.

Nadine Miller
International Studies
Rochester, N.Y.

Pamela Miller
Psychology
Morrison, Ill.

Walter Miller
Electronics Technology
Bloomingdale, Ill.

Aubrey Millet
Biology
Chicago, Ill.

Robert Mitchell
Accounting
Watseka, Ill.

Robert Mollis
Electronics Technology
E. Moline, Ill.

Rosiland Moredock
Speech & Hearing
Peoria, Ill.

Barbara Moretto
Elementary Education
Peoria, Ill.

James Moroz
Electrical Engineering
Joliet, Ill.

Patricia Morrison
Sociology
Geneva, N.Y.

Carol Mower
Elementary Education
Galesburg, Ill.

Paul Mroz
Biology
Chicago, Ill.

Joyce Muller
Music
E. Peoria, Ill.

James Munchoff
Industrial Engineering
Western Springs, Ill.

Dale Murawski
Mathematics
Mt. Prospect, Ill.

Joyce Murphy
English
Lake Villa, Ill.

Roslyn Murphy
History
Pekin, Ill.

Therese Naddy
Psychology
Chicago, Ill.

Harry Nappie
Engine Power Technology
Peoria, Ill.

Matthew Nardi
Political Science
Peapack, N.J.

David Nell
Mathematics
Peoria, Ill.

Charles Nelson
Mathematics
Round Lake, Ill.

Don Nelson
Mechanical Engineering
Lewistown, Ill.

Ellen Nelson
Sociology
Peoria, Ill.

Richard Nelson
Biology
Lake Forest, Ill.

Thomas Nelson
Accounting
Elmhurst, Ill.

Walter Neumann
Civil Engineering
Bridgview, Ill.

David Nykiel
Civil Engineering
Chicago, Ill.

Annette Ochakolf
Elementary Education
Chicago, Ill.

Russ O'Connor
Construction Technology
Andes, N.Y.

Terry O'Connor
Elementary Education
Peoria, Ill.

Claudia Olech
Elementary Education
Oak Park, Ill.

William Oliver
Industrial Engineering
LaGrange, Ill.

Donald Olson
Mechanical Engineering
Peoria, Ill.

Richard Olson
Art
Maywood, Ill.

David Olszak
Construction Technology
Crystal Lake, Ill.

James Otten
Electrical Engineering
Peoria, Ill.

Roger Ouellette
Physical Education
Peoria, Ill.

Carol Ozaga
History
Chicago, Ill.

Lee Owen
Retailing & Marketing
Cedarburg, Wis.

Gary Pace
Psychology
Chicago, Ill.

Virginia Pack
Chemistry
Morris, Ill.

Peggy Paetsch
Elementary Education
Blue Island, Ill.

Robert Paige
History
Stamford, Conn.

Francie Paller
Sociology
University Heights, O.

Sarah Palmer
Elementary Education
Meridian, Ga.

Dru Pardieck
Art
Hinsdale, Ill.

Henry Patterson
Business Man. & Admin.
Rockford, Ill.

Lenard Pearlman
Retailing & Marketing
Highland Park, Ill.

Ross Penny
Mathematics
Alton, Ill.

Michael Perelstein
Economics
St. Paul, Minn.

Shirley Perley
Elementary Education
Peoria, Ill.

Judith Peters
Elementary Education
Peoria, Ill.

William Peterson
Electrical Engineering
Rockford, Ill.

Camille Petriska
Home Economics
Burnham, Ill.

Eugene Petrovits
Mechanical Engineering
Chicago, Ill.

Gerald Pfeiffer
Accounting
Ashton, Ill.

Frank Pikul
Biology
E. St. Louis, Ill.

Mary Pittman
Psychology
Flora, Ill.

Bruce Plassmeyer
Sociology
Evanston, Ill.

Michael Poirot
Engine Power Technology
Belleville, Ill.

Donna Pollack
Retailing & Marketing
Downers Grove, Ill.

Sharon Pollack
Speech & Hearing
Downers Grove, Ill.

Troy Pombert
Retailing & Marketing
Kankakee, Ill.

Gary Pon
Engine Power Technology
Baltimore, Md.

Jerome Pope
Political Science
Evergreen Park, Ill.

Rochelle Portee
Sociology
New York, N.Y.

Bernadette Potempa
Sociology
Chicago, Ill.

Donald Potempa
Accounting
Olympia Fields, Ill.

Lawrence Potempa
Biology
Chicago, Ill.

James Pottorf
Journalism
Mason City, Ill.

David Pounds
Biology
Peoria, Ill.

JoAnn Powell
Retailing & Marketing
Fort Worth, Tex.

Judith Preskill
Art
Peoria, Ill.

Roy Prohaska
Construction Technology
Chicago, Ill.

Charles Puffer
Business Man. & Admin.
Woodstock, Conn.

Nancy Purdy
International Studies
Libertyville, Ill.

Rhonda Rabins
Sociology
Skokie, Ill.

Stanley Radosevich
Political Science
Peoria, Ill.

Terry Ramsey
Electrical Engineering
Mattoon, Ill.

250

Andrew Randall
Business Man. & Admin.
Stamford, Conn.

Thomas Ranieri
Philosophy
Chicago Heights, Ill.

William Ransdell
Biology
Libertyville, Ill.

James Rasmussen
Accounting
Batavia, Ill.

Gail Rayford
Psychology
Chicago, Ill.

Bonita Raymond
Journalism
Chicago, Ill.

Mary Record
Physical Education
Decatur, Ill.

Randall Redard
Psychology
Tenafly, N.J.

Peter Reimann
Construction Technology
Elmhurst, Ill.

Barry Redenbo
International Studies
E. Peoria, Ill.

Charles Reiss
Psychology
Sheboygan, Wis.

Richard Render
Electronics Technology
Westchester, Ill.

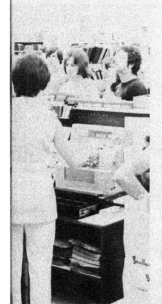

Carl Renouard
Mathematics
Westmont, Ill.

Jane Rheinwald
Journalism
Peoria, Ill.

Randy Rhodes
Electronics Technology
Owego, N.Y.

Robert Ringness
Mechanical Engineering
Peoria, Ill.

Jacqueline Ripka
Psychology
Peoria, Ill.

Lawrence Ritchie
Electrical Engineering
Rock Falls, Ill.

Caroline Roberts
Art
Lake Forest, Ill.

Lona Roberts
Retailing & Marketing
Chicago, Ill.

Marcia Roberts
Elementary Education
Peoria, Ill.

Marcie Robin
Elementary Education
Chicago, Ill.

Cathy Robinowitz
Special Education
Hartsdale, N.Y.

Susan Robinson
Elementary Education
Trenton, N.J.

251

Peter Roblin
Business Man. & Admin.
Newton, Mass.

Michael Romano
History
Chicago, Ill.

Sally Roscher
Art
Lake Bluff, Ill.

Suzanne Rose
Psychology
Peoria, Ill.

David Rosen
Speech
Skokie, Ill.

Nello Rossi
Psychology
Manito, Ill.

Paul Royer
Electronics Technology
Mt. Prospect, Ill.

Ronald Rubin
Political Science
Morton Grove, Ill.

Ralph Russell
Engine Power Technology
Riverside, Ill.

Roger Ruthhart
Journalism
Barrington, Ill.

Brian Rutkie
Physical Education
Euclid, O.

Cathy Sabin
Elementary Education
Evanston, Ill.

Dennis Saffrin
Accounting
Wilmette, Ill.

Margaret Sagil
French
Chicago, Ill.

Keith Salems
Chemistry
Morris, Ill.

Daniel Salrin
Accounting
Mt. Sterling, Ill.

Lynn Salvatori
English
Villa Park, Ill.

Gail Samos
Speech
Lincolnwood, Ill.

James Sartori
Economics
Riverdale, Ill.

Clark Sauer
Construction Technology
Phoenix, Ariz.

Kathleen Schafer
Art
Bayville, N.J.

Edward Schavitz
Construction Technology
Arlington Heights, Ill.

Melvin Schlentner
Mathematics
Pittsburgh, Pa.

Nancy Schmidt
Spanish
Chicago, Ill.

James Schneff
Business Man. & Admin.
Elgin, Ill.

Patricia Schnitker
Art
Centralia, Ill.

Jeffrey Schonbrun
Biology
Schaumburg, Ill.

Karen Schulte
History
St. Louis, Mo.

Wayne Schupp
Retailing & Marketing
Elgin, Ill.

Gregory Schwarting
Business Man. & Admin.
Evergreen Park, Ill.

Lauren Schwartz
English
University Heights, O.

Sally Seher
Home Economics
Barrington, Ill.

Daniel Seitz
Electrical Engineering
Peoria, Ill.

Stuart Septimus
Psychology
N. Woodmere, N.Y.

Jeffrey Serle
Sociology
Flushing, N.Y.

Lynn Shade
Elementary Education
Franklin Park, Ill.

Paul Shapiro
Accounting
Old Bethpage, N.Y.

Charles Sharp
Business Man. & Admin.
Elwood, Ill.

Mary Ellen Sheinbein
Elementary Education
Olivette, Mo.

James Sherrill
Accounting
Hamilton, Ill.

Bernice Shevitz
Speech Pathology
Plainview, N.Y.

Melvin Shoup
Accounting
Peoria, Ill.

Sheila Shrader
Music Education
Princeville, Ill.

William Shuter
Engine Power Technology
Northport, N.J.

Jack Sills
Biology
Chicago, Ill.

Cindy Siokos
Elementary Education
Elmwood Park, Ill.

Craig Sjurset
Business Man. & Admin.
Elgin, Ill.

Deborah Skalsky
Elementary Education
Chicago, Ill.

Richard Skirball
Psychology
Granite City, Ill.

Michael Sklar
Sociology
West Orange, N.J.

Jennifer Slack
Elementary Education
St. Joseph, Mo.

Jeffrey Small
English & History
Waterbury, Conn.

253

Ted Small
Business Man. & Admin.
Mt. Prospect, Ill.

Brian Smith
Political Science
Norridge, Ill.

Carl Smith
Accounting
Hanna City, Ill.

Ethel Smith
Special Education
Peoria, Ill.

Rodger Smith
Engine Power Technology
Virden, Ill.

Rodney Smith
Engine Power Technology
Bristol, R.I.

Deborah Snedeker
French
Peoria, Ill.

Donald Snyder
Accounting
Geneva, Ill.

Carol Socha
History
Chicago, Ill.

Nancy Somers
Sociology
Lynchburg, Va.

Larry Sorensen
Psychology
Evergreen Park, Ill.

William Sorensen
Mathematics
Rockford, Ill.

Anthony Sparacio
Physical Education
Dumont, N.J.

Shelley Spark
Biology
Highland Park, Ill.

Sheila Spear
Elementary Education
Calumet City, Ill.

Alana Stahl
Mathematics
Peoria, Ill.

Michael Stanis
Mathematics
Riverside, R.I.

Reid Stanton
Philosophy
Evanston, Ill.

Douglas Steele
Psychology
Kankakee, Ill.

Patti Steffens
Elementary Education
Wilmette, Ill.

Collette Steg
Physical Education
Jamestown, N.Y.

Tomme Stevenson
Business Man. & Admin.
Marseilles, Ill.

William Strauss
Music Business
Peoria, Ill.

Susan Streitmatter
Elementary Education
Princeville, Ill.

Anita Strom
Elementary Education
Lincolnwood, Ill.

Clifford Strom
Sociology
Des Plaines, Ill.

Neal Strom
Political Science
Wilmette, Ill.

Mark Stuart
History
River Vale, N.J.

William Stuart
Mathematics
Kankakee, Ill.

John Swan
Electronics Technology
East Moline, Ill.

William Sweasy
Business Man. & Admin.
Peoria, Ill.

Charles Tarjan
English
Riverdale, Ill.

Robyn Tarshes
Art
Chicago, Ill.

Robert T. Taylor
Electrical Engineering
Arlington Heights, Ill.

Robert W. Taylor
Engine Power Technology
Waukegan, Ill.

Marsha Tedford
English
Elburn, Ill.

Brian Telander
Business Man. & Admin.
Evergreen Park, Ill.

Raymond Theis
Electrical Engineering
Burlington, Ia.

Dorothy Theobald
Home Economics
E. Peoria, Ill.

Phyllis Thomas
Chemistry
Lisle, Ill.

Stephen Tiber
History
Kansas City, Mo.

Gordon Tingley
Electrical Engineering
Vermont, Ill.

Brian Tischendorf
Industrial Engineering
Libertyville, Ill.

Ralph Tisher
Engine Power Technology
Leadington, Mo.

Cathy Tivol
Psychology
Shawnee Mission, Ka.

Jack Tollefson
Electronics Technology
Peoria, Ill.

Mark Tollefson
Physics
Peoria, Ill.

Erika Tomczyk
German
Erie, Pa.

Robert Topal
Sociology
Brooklyn, N.Y.

Mary Tracy
Psychology
Princeville, Ill.

Janice Tucker
Speech & Hearing
Chicago, Ill.

Andria Tun
Elementary Education
Des Plaines, Ill.

John Underwood
Political Science
Chicago, Ill.

Mary Utley
Elementary Education
Peoria, Ill.

Rose Venovich
Business Man. & Admin.
Pekin, Ill.

Randi Viner
Sociology
Chicago, Ill.

Craig Vinke
Business Man. & Admin.
South Holland, Ill.

James Vogt
Business Man. & Admin.
Oak Park, Ill.

Eugene Voss
Psychology
Peoria, Ill.

Ira Waldschmidt
Accounting
Peoria, Ill.

Gary Wallington
Geology
Peoria, Ill.

Jan Wanack
Music Education
Tremont, Ill.

George Wargo
Electrical Engineering
Benld, Ill.

Carl Warren
Engine Power Technology
Chicago, Ill.

Gail Warren
History
Chicago, Ill.

Addison Watanabe
Biology
Peoria, Ill.

Charles Waterbury
Electronics Technology
Larchmont, N.Y.

Stephen Watkins
French
Peoria, Ill.

Pamela Watts
Home Economics
Peoria, Ill.

Carla Weckel
Elementary Education
North Pont, N.J.

Thomas Weed
Economics
Peoria, Ill.

Sandra Weiss
Elementary Education
Merrick, N.Y.

William Wendle
Business Man. & Admin.
Peoria, Ill.

David West
Business Man. & Admin.
Peoria, Ill.

Kent West
Business Man. & Admin.
Decatur, Ill.

Lester Whaley
Business Man. & Admin.
E. Peoria, Ill.

George Wheeler
Engine Power Technology
Henry, Ill.

John Whitcomb
Economics
Palatine, Ill.

Robert Wicke
History
Huntley, Ill.

Gregory Wieczorek
Physics
Oak Park, Ill.

Valerie Wilcoxson
History
E. Peoria, Ill.

Dennis Williams
Business Man. & Admin.
Evergreen Park, Ill.

Eugene Williams
Psychology
Peoria, Ill.

Gary Wilson
Mathematics
Peoria, Ill.

Lee Wilson
International Studies
Libertyville, Ill.

Stephen Wipert
Business Man. & Admin.
Peoria, Ill.

Susan Wise
Mathematics
Dunlap, Ill.

John Witthuhn
Electrical Engineering
Elgin, Ill.

Michele Wohlschlegel
Home Economics
Peoria, Ill.

Sandee Wolpin
Physical Education
Chicago, Ill.

Joseph Wood
Chemistry
Danville, Ill.

Paula Woolf
Elementary Education
Peoria, Ill.

Fredrica Worlds
Mathematics
Chicago, Ill.

Frederick Wrieden
Construction Technology
Gaithersburg, Md.

Claire Wrobel
English
Lincolnwood, Ill.

Alan Yates
Psychology
Centerport, N.Y.

Michael Yazbec
Civil Engineering
Milan, Ill.

Carolyn Young
Elementary Education
Honolulu, Hi.

Jean Young
Psychology
Evanston, Ill.

Beth Zelden
Speech
Chicago, Ill.

Joseph Zeman
Mechanical Engineering
Paw Paw, Ill.

Dessy Zirinis
French
Des Plaines, Ill.

Richard Zuckerman
Political Science
Skokie, Ill.

Robert Zyskowski
Journalism
Chicago, Ill.

257

INDEX

staFF

Editor-in-chief . . . .Barbara Salins
Assistant Editor . . . . .Laura Judd
Managing Editor . . .Miriam Smith
Photography Editor .Phillip Ceraulo
Assistant Photo Editor .Steve Glaser
Student Life . . . . .Diana Robbins
Staff . . . . .Greg Goyen
Competition . . .Randy Worcester
Staff . . . . .Pete Odon
Habitations . . . . . .Kathy Golob
Participation . . . .Brenda Fleming
Marybeth Genis
Individuals . . . . . .Peggy Butler
Staff . . . . . .Mary Anne Potts
Marie Saul
Index . . . . .Monica Avery
Cover design and division page
lettering . . . . .Mike Dore
Contributing photographers . . . . .
Audio Visual Department
John Baird
Mark Belokon
Bruce Cohen
Mark Eidinger
Mike Gebben, Scout Photo Editor
Tom Gold
Ann Lewan
Howard Meiseles
Patricia Moore
Peter Ogden
Gerald Shaffner
Charles Sharp
Business Manager . .Wayne Schupp
Advisor . . . . .Dr. William Steiner
Delmar Printing Company
. . . . .Mr. Ed Hackleman
Mr. Mike Hackleman
Root Photography Studio .Mr. Scott
Nozawa

Help Wanted

Small yearbook with experienced
staff seeks advisor to go down with
sinking ship. Qualifications: able
to counsel editor about deadlines,
love life, women's lib, inner feelings
and emotions, classes and professors, and life in general. Must not
interfere or censor book, must attend all pub council meetings, drop
in occasionally to say hello to staff,
and handle all financial hassles.
Apply in person.

The 1973 **Anaga** was published at Bradley
University, Peoria, Illinois, and printed
through offset lithography by Delmar Printing
Company, Charlotte, North Carolina. The 264
pages were printed on 80 lb. Northwest
Mounty Matte. Division pages were printed
on solar yellow cover weight stock. Headline
type is 24 pt. optima italic, body copy is 10/12
optima, and cutlines are 8/9 optima italic. The
cover is a three color custom litho designed
by Mike Dore and processed by Delmar.
There are 8 pages of Deltone color process.
Press run of 2,000 copies. Address all inquiries
to **Anaga** Office, Student Center, Bradley
University, Peoria, Illinois 61606.

Published by authority of the Publications Council of Bradley University

CPSIA information can be obtained
at www.ICGtesting.com
Printed in the USA
BVHW04*1343180918
527831BV00012B/646/P